California
Bar
Examination

Performance Tests
and
Selected Answers

February 2016

The State Bar Of California
Committee of Bar Examiners/Office of Admissions

180 Howard Street • San Francisco, CA 94105-1639 • (415) 538-2300
845 S. Figueroa Street • Los Angeles, CA 90017-2515 • (213) 765-1500

PERFORMANCE TESTS AND SELECTED ANSWERS

FEBRUARY 2016

CALIFORNIA BAR EXAMINATION

This publication contains two performance tests from the February 2016 California Bar Examination and two selected answers for each test.

The answers were assigned high grades and were written by applicants who passed the examination after one read. The answers were produced as submitted by the applicant, except that minor corrections in spelling and punctuation were made for ease in reading. They are reproduced here with the consent of the authors.

CONTENTS

February 2016

California Bar Examination

Performance Test A

INSTRUCTIONS AND FILE

IN THE MATTER OF MILLY NOLAN FLECK

IN THE MATTER OF MILLY NOLAN FLECK

INSTRUCTIONS

1. This performance test is designed to evaluate your ability to handle a select number of legal authorities in the context of a factual problem involving a client.

2. The problem is set in the fictional State of Columbia, one of the United States.

3. You will have two sets of materials with which to work: a File and a Library.

4. The File contains factual materials about your case. The first document is a memorandum containing the instructions for the tasks you are to complete.

5. The Library contains the legal authorities needed to complete the tasks. The case reports may be real, modified, or written solely for the purpose of this performance test. If the cases appear familiar to you, do not assume that they are precisely the same as you have read before. Read each thoroughly, as if it were new to you. You should assume that cases were decided in the jurisdictions and on the dates shown. In citing cases from the Library, you may use abbreviations and omit page citations.

6. You should concentrate on the materials provided, but you should also bring to bear on the problem your general knowledge of the law. What you have learned in law school and elsewhere provides the general background for analyzing the problem; the File and Library provide the specific materials with which you must work.

7. Although there are no parameters on how to apportion your time, you should allow yourself sufficient time to thoroughly review the materials and organize your planned response.

8. Your response will be graded on its compliance with instructions and on its content, thoroughness, and organization.

OFFICE OF CHIEF TRIAL COUNSEL

STATE BAR OF COLUMBIA

TO: Applicant

FROM: Chief Trial Counsel

DATE: February 23, 2016

SUBJECT: In the Matter of Milly Nolan Fleck, Respondent

We have completed our investigation and are ready to decide whether to file charges against respondent Milly Nolan Fleck. The investigation arose out of claims made by a client Fleck represented. Ms. Liora Hersh asserted that Fleck had misappropriated and withheld $500 from a personal injury settlement. During discovery there came to light a problem resulting from the negligent handling of Fleck's client trust account (CTA). Fleck may have commingled her own funds in her CTA, and it appears that the balance in Fleck's CTA fell below the amount it should minimally have contained for a period of six weeks. We have double-checked the investigator's CTA reconciliation, and it is accurate.

The State Bar investigator has recommended that we charge Fleck with violations of:

1. Rule 4-100(A) for failure to maintain appropriate funds in her CTA;

2. Rule 4-100(B) for failing to promptly pay funds to a client;

3. Rule 4-100(A) for commingling her own funds in her CTA: and

4. Section 6068 for failure to cooperate with a disciplinary investigation.

Prepare a memorandum evaluating whether we can prevail on each of these charges.

OFFICE OF CHIEF TRIAL COUNSEL

STATE BAR OF COLUMBIA

SUBJECT: In the Matter of Milly Nolan Fleck, Respondent

FROM: Ignacio Gomez, Investigator

Interview of Complaining Party (Liora Hersh)

On June 23, 2015, Liora Hersh (Hersh) filed a complaint against Milly Nolan Fleck (Fleck).

Fleck has been an active member of the State Bar of Columbia since May 2009.

In October 2013, Liora Hersh, a paralegal, employed Fleck to represent her on a contingency basis in a personal injury matter. Hersh did not execute the written agreement prepared and sent to her by Fleck for such representation. [I reviewed it, a standard personal injury contingent fee agreement, and Hersh does not dispute its terms.]

Several weeks later, Hersh asked Fleck to handle a separate child custody matter. Fleck and Hersh discussed the fees for the handling of the child custody matter, including Fleck's usual requirement of a retainer plus monthly payments. Fleck wanted a retainer of $500 as an advance on fees that would be incurred. Because Hersh told Fleck that she could not provide a retainer, Fleck offered to handle the child custody matter if Hersh would make her best efforts to pay the monthly bills and if Fleck could use the anticipated recovery from the personal injury matter for the retainer and to pay off any unpaid balance in the child custody matter. Hersh agreed, and she employed Fleck in the child custody matter.

Shortly thereafter, Fleck sent Hersh a written agreement that set forth Fleck's fee at an hourly rate, but did not mention the use of the proceeds from the recovery in the personal injury matter to satisfy any unpaid fees in the child custody matter. Hersh did not sign the agreement for the child custody matter. Fleck billed her monthly, but Hersh did not make regular payments for Fleck's work. Hersh did, however, express satisfaction with Fleck's efforts on her behalf and sent payments to Fleck in December 2013 and in January, May, August, and October 2014.

In April 2014, Fleck met with Hersh to discuss possible settlement of her personal injury action. Hersh again agreed that Fleck could take a retainer of $500 and pay off the outstanding balance in the child custody matter out of the anticipated recovery in her personal injury matter.

On October 29, 2014, Fleck settled the personal injury matter for $17,500. Fleck called Hersh and notified her of the settlement on that day.   Hersh indicated that the settlement was very satisfactory, and in fact was $5,000 more than she had anticipated and earlier approved.

A few days later, Hersh received from Fleck's office the $17,500 settlement check made out to Fleck and Hersh for endorsement.

At first she did not sign the check. Hersh had two telephone conversations about the distribution of the settlement from the personal injury matter with Larry Gold, a secretary or assistant in Fleck's office. In the first conversation, Hersh challenged the intended deduction of the retainer and overdue fees in the child custody matter, asserting that she considered them to be totally separate matters. Gold said that he would talk to Fleck and call her back. A few days later, Gold called Hersh and reminded her of her agreement permitting Fleck to deduct the fees. Gold also said that no prior attempt had been made to collect the fees owed in the child custody matter because of the agreement. When Hersh asked to speak with Fleck, Gold said that Fleck did not want to talk with her. Gold explained that if Hersh disagreed about the deduction of the fees in the child custody matter from the recovery in the personal injury matter, she could refuse to sign the check and could come to the office to talk directly with Fleck. At the end of the conversation, Hersh said, "Okay, go ahead and distribute it." Hersh said that she would endorse the settlement check, but insisted that Fleck distribute the funds as quickly as possible. Hersh signed the check and returned it to Fleck's office.

A week later, Hersh received a check and a letter from Fleck. The letter (dated November 28, 2014) explained the distribution. The check covered the balance remaining after the deduction of all costs in the personal injury matter, Fleck's one-third contingency fee in the personal injury matter, the unpaid amount owed by Hersh in the child custody matter, and a retainer ($500) for future work on the child custody matter. The letter also stated that Fleck would refund the $500 retainer if Hersh sent back a signed form for substitution of attorney. Hersh was not surprised that Fleck offered to withdraw from the child custody case after she had disputed the distribution. Hersh signed and cashed the check. Hersh never objected to the distribution of the personal injury settlement described in the letter. Hersh confirmed that she never communicated any retraction, oral or written, of the authorization she gave by telephone to distribute the funds.

A couple of months later, Hersh had second thoughts, and realized that in effect she had both paid off everything due to Fleck and another $500, that she had called a retainer. The contingent fee Fleck had obtained from their settlement should have been a sufficient retainer. She felt she was taken advantage of and overcharged. Hersh decided to change lawyers. Hersh's employer said he'd finish the custody case, and charge her only if fees exceeded $500. On February 26, 2015, Hersh signed and sent Fleck the substitution of attorney, and in a brief letter Hersh asked Fleck to sign and return the substitution and to refund the $500 retainer as soon as possible.

A little later Hersh received the signed substitution, but Fleck did not include the $500. Hersh claims that Fleck has failed to return the $500 retainer despite repeated requests. Hersh sent Fleck three letters demanding that she return the $500. Fleck has been withholding the $500 for almost 6 months, and she concluded that Fleck intends to keep it.

Milly Nolan Fleck

Attorney at Law

1959 Stingray Boulevard

yourattorney@millynolanfleck.com

Reunion, Columbia

November 28, 2014

Liora Hersh

P.O. Box 3333

Reunion, Columbia

Dear Liora,

Thank you for your cooperation in resolving the possible conflict. I am pleased to be able to enclose the check settling your claims in the personal injury case.

The settlement was for $17,500. From that amount, I have deducted the following:

1. My contingent fee of $5,775.

2. The pending unpaid balance due in your child custody case of $2,250, previously billed to you.

3.   My retainer of $500 against future fees, for handling the custody matter.

The balance to you is $8,975, and my check in that amount is enclosed.

Also, I am enclosing another copy of the Release of All Claims I previously sent you for signing. It should have been returned with the check for the full settlement. As you know, we must provide the release to the insurance company as a condition of the settlement and as a condition of signing the check for your recovery. Please sign and return in the enclosed, stamped envelope.

Finally, in case the recent exchanges with my office indicate a dissatisfaction with my services, I have enclosed a Substitution of Attorney in the custody matter. All you need to do is sign and return it, and you are free to obtain another counsel. Then, I will of course refund the retainer.

Best wishes,

Milly Fleck

Milly Nolan Fleck

MEMORANDUM

OFFICE OF CHIEF TRIAL COUNSEL

Telephone Interview of Respondent (Milly Nolan Fleck), October 15, 2015

QUESTION [Ignacio Gomez]: Okay, thank you Ms. Fleck. I have turned on the tape recorder to record our interview.

ANSWER [Milly Fleck]: That's fine, Mr. Gomez. I simply don't have time to come down to your office, now that I have started working at a new job at this firm. I have shut down my private practice, completed or handed off all my cases and clients, and don't really understand why the State Bar is pursuing this petty complaint. I take my obligations as an attorney very seriously and was always available for my clients. I gave 150% for my clients, and Liora Hersh was at the top of that list. What more could she want?

Q: I do have questions, especially since you didn't respond to our notices about the Hersh complaint. Notices were sent to you after the Hersh complaint, one dated June 28, 2015, another one dated July 20, 2015, and another August 30, 2015.

A: I didn't get them. The office was closed. The mail was forwarded to a Columbia Mail Boxes, Inc. office, and I was picking it up every week or so, but your notices apparently arrived when I was not checking often, and then I took a needed break to be with my mother for a couple of months. The first I heard about the Hersh complaint was when you called me here at the firm last month, after I sent my new address to the State Bar.

Q: Yes, but it was after four months. You are obligated to keep your address current.

A: I am obligated to my clients and I took care of those obligations, Mr. Gomez. I have a pre-trial conference this morning. Can we get to the complaint? Liora didn't like that I kept the $500 retainer that she agreed to, and then that I held it because she would not sign the release. Is that it?

Q: You held the money for many months, even after you had withdrawn as her lawyer. What's this about the release?

A: I sent her the full settlement check, with the release from the insurance company. After first trying to back out of their agreement, Liora told Larry -- Larry Gold, my assistant -- that she would sign and return both. The $500 was my retainer, against future fees. She hadn't been paying monthly as promised. But I had told Larry not to attempt to collect the large outstanding bill in the child custody matter because of her agreement to pay the balance owed out of anticipated recovery in the personal injury matter. Then, that money came in, and Liora didn't want to pay. That was a red flag that we had problems, and so I offered to withdraw and let her get a new lawyer. She did so, but she just wouldn't sign the release, and the insurance company kept asking for it, even after I had dismissed the case. I sent Liora several letters about the release. Did she tell you that?

Q: Well, I didn't know that the release was a problem. Is that why you kept her money?

A: Yes. The only reason. We worked out the distribution of the settlement, I thought, but she decided to switch lawyers, which was okay with me, but for some reason, she just would not sign and return the release. I still don't know why. It still isn't signed, and I guess the insurer has just forgotten or let it go.

Q: But you know that, pursuant to the rules, once you signed the substitution and had withdrawn you must promptly refund any unearned fees, and the $500 was unearned fees.

A: I kept it, to try to encourage Liora to sign the release. She was obligated by the settlement to sign it, and I was concerned about the possibility of a motion for compliance with the terms of the settlement. Technically, she was not entitled to any of the proceeds until she had signed the release.

Q: Don't you think it was reasonable for Hersh to think that you were withholding the $500 because of the admittedly deteriorated relationship with her?

A: Absolutely not. Liora was savvy, and she was probably holding the release to pressure me, not the other way around.

Q: You closed your private practice in June 2015.

A: Yes. I spent much of March and April helping my father with his business. He had a terminal illness, and was in and out of the hospital during this period until his death in late April 2015. I ran his business in addition to my own practice through May 2015.

Q: You started your present job in early September 2015?

A: Yes, just a few weeks ago.

Q: You did not send the $500 to Ms. Hersh until after I first called you last month?

A: Yes. I had forgotten about it, probably after the insurance company gave up, and the funds sat there in my client trust account.

Q: May I ask you about your client trust account?

A: Yes. Larry told me you looked at the records and asked him about it.

Q: You kept track of your client trust account?

A: Yes. Larry helped, but I signed any withdrawal, kept my own ledger of the CTA, and would reconcile my ledger with the bank records periodically, at least annually.

Q: Did you do that at the end of 2014?

A: No, not then. Between my father's illness and his business, I didn't get to it. Also, I knew that there had been very few deposits and withdrawals from late 2014 until I closed the practice, and I thought everything was in order.

Q: I noticed that during that time your client trust account had $125 that doesn't appear to have been from any client. Was that your money?

A: Let me think. Oh, yes, when I opened a new trust account, I added about $125. I thought we needed new checks and a new check ledger, and kept that there to pay for them.

Q: $125, for checks?

A: Yes. The ledger was leather, and I anticipated that it and the checks would cost over $100.

Q: Ms. Fleck, in view of the months of delay in responding, and now only talking by phone, could you please come in to our office for a more extensive review?

A: I really can't. Feel free to call me. Mr. Gold will meet if necessary. My files are open to you. But really, this is only about a client who became disgruntled about the deal she made, and is now using the State Bar complaint process to undo the agreement.

Q: Well, if you will not come in, then we will leave it there for the moment.

MEMORANDUM

OFFICE OF CHIEF TRIAL COUNSEL

STATE BAR OF COLUMBIA

SUBJECT: **Examination of Respondent's Records**

In the Matter of Milly Nolan Fleck, Respondent

FROM: Ignacio Gomez, Investigator

On October 1, 2015, Larry Gold came to the office to drop off Milly Nolan Fleck's correspondence file with Liora Hersh, and the records of Fleck's client trust bank account (CTA) for 2014 and 2015 (which I had asked for to determine what had been done with Hersh's $500 before it was returned to her).

Mr. Gold appeared to freely answer my questions, and he volunteered that Fleck had asked him to cooperate in any way -- "to get it over with," he quotes her as saying.

Mr. Gold confirmed Hersh's version of his two telephone conversations with her in November 2014, although he characterized Hersh's tone as "emotional, dramatic, and unprofessional for a paralegal." Hersh agreed to cover the unpaid fees and the $500 retainer by letting Fleck deduct them from the settlement. Fleck instructed him to prepare the accounting and cut the checks, and he did so immediately.

Mr. Gold was in charge of Fleck's clients' trust, operating and payroll bank accounts. However, he said that Fleck herself would sign any withdrawals from the client trust account, and she would reconcile and double-check the CTA.

Fleck had just switched banks, and opened a new CTA for all client funds. After they received the signed settlement check back from Hersh, Gold deposited the $17,500 in the new account. He deducted Fleck's contingent fee ($5,775), the unpaid balance due in the child custody case, $2,250 (for 15 hours at $150 / hr), and the $500 retainer, and prepared a check for Fleck's signature to Hersh for the balance of $8,975. He then transferred the contingent fee and unpaid fees to Fleck's operating account. Fleck signed and sent the check, and okayed the transfers.

Gold's explanation should have meant a balance of $500 in Fleck's new CTA. However, on December 31, 2014, the total balance in Fleck's new trust account was $625. This balance represented the $500 retainer for future work on the child custody case plus another $125 (later determined to be Fleck's own funds, commingled in the CTA, below).

On February 18, 2015, Fleck deposited a check for $250 from Client A into this trust account. On March 19, 2015, Fleck wrote a check drawn on the CTA to Client A for $385. Although Fleck did not realize it at the time, this check reduced the balance in the trust account to $490 when it cleared on March 27, 2015.

I asked Mr. Gold about it, and he said, "It was a mistake." They had received two checks from Client A, each for $250, but he had mistakenly thought only one was an advance and deposited only one of the checks in the CTA, and the other in the operating account. Fleck had assumed that both checks were deposited into the CTA, and that there was a balance of $500 for the credit of Client A in the CTA.

However, when Fleck wrote the $385 check to Client A on March 19, 2015, it was obvious from the face of the statement from the bank that the new trust account did not contain both deposits on behalf of Client A. It should have been patently obvious that the balance would dip below the $500 that Fleck had received as a retainer from Hersh. From March 27, 2015, to April 30, 2015, the balance in Fleck's trust account remained at $490, slightly less than the $500 that Fleck should have kept in it. On April 30, 2015, a $4,807 deposit from another matter raised the balance in the account to $5,297.

I have prepared and attached a reconciliation if it would help. However, there can be no doubt that from March 27, 2015 until April 30, 2015, the balance in Fleck's CTA was $490, below the requisite balance of the $500 due to Hersh.

It did not appear that Fleck ever determined on her own that a trust account problem had occurred. I believe she realized this for the first time when I called and told her about it after my review. Gold was responsible for making deposits into the operating account, and Fleck did not inspect the checks that went into the operating account. The misdeposit was the first of a series of events that eventually caused the balance in Fleck's trust account to fall below the necessary amount. Thus, the $250 misdeposit from Client A remained undetected.

It is my conclusion, from these records, that Fleck committed a violation of Rule 4-100(A) because she negligently failed to keep in her trust account the entire $500 held for Ms. Hersh.

It also appears that the commingling of $125 of Fleck's personal funds is a clear violation.

The correspondence file confirmed Fleck's assertion that, in each letter she sent to Hersh after the settlement, she asked her to sign and return the release. There were three letters solely requesting the release. In all, Fleck made written requests to Hersh for the signed release seven times, and sent her copies of the release in three of the requests. Her files included three requests to her from the insurance company's counsel for the release. However, Fleck made no more efforts since concluding her practice, and retained Hersh's money until she learned about her complaint from my contact. I conclude that Fleck improperly failed to refund the advance fee.

Fleck failed to keep the State Bar informed of her current address, did not respond to our inquiries, and is reluctant to meet. This has hampered further investigation, and forced me to conclude the matter and refer it to the Chief Trial Counsel.

State Bar Investigator's Reconciliation

of Millie Nolan Fleck's CTA

			CTA Balance
11/28/14:	Fleck opens new CTA and deposits check in settlement of Hersh PI case	$17,500	$17,500
11/28/14:	Check to Fleck's operating account (contingent fee)	$5,775	$11,725
11/28/14:	Check to Fleck's operating account (billed/ unpaid fees for Hersh child custody matter)	$2,250	$9,475
11/28/14:	Check to Hersh for balance of settlement	$8,975	$500
12/15/14:	Unidentified deposit by Fleck	$125	$625
2/18/15:	Deposit of "advance" from Client A	$250	$875
3/27/15:	Check to Client A cleared bank	$385	$490
4/30/15:	Deposit from another Fleck case	$4,807	$5,297

February 2016

California
Bar
Examination

Performance Test A
LIBRARY

IN THE MATTER OF MILLY NOLAN FLECK

LIBRARY

SELECTED PROVISIONS OF

COLUMBIA PROFESSIONS CODE

AND

COLUMBIA RULES OF PROFESSIONAL CONDUCT

Columbia Professions Code

Section 6068

It is the duty of an attorney to cooperate and participate in any disciplinary investigation or other regulatory or disciplinary proceeding pending against himself or herself.

Columbia Rules of Professional Conduct

Rule 3-700. Termination of Employment

(A)   In General.

*   *   *   *   *

(D)   Papers, Property, and Fees. A member whose employment has terminated shall:

*   *   *   *   *

    (2)   Promptly refund any part of a fee paid in advance that has not been earned. This provision is not applicable to a true retainer fee which is paid solely for the purpose of ensuring the availability of the member for the matter.

Discussion:

Paragraph (D) also requires that the member "promptly" return unearned fees paid in advance. Further, Paragraph D(2) recognizes the validity of true retainers, and is consistent with the Columbia Supreme Court's definition of a retainer: "A retainer is a sum of money paid by a client to secure an attorney's availability over a given period of time. Thus, such a fee is earned by the attorney when paid since the attorney is entitled to the money regardless of whether he actually performs any services for the client." *Baranowski v. State Bar* (1979). However, an advance against future fees is not a retainer, even if denominated as a "retainer" or even a "non-refundable retainer."

Rule 4-100. Preserving Identity of Funds and Property of a Client

(A) All funds received or held for the benefit of clients by a member or law firm, including advances for costs and expenses, shall be deposited in one or more identifiable bank accounts labeled "Trust Account," "Client's Funds Account" or words of similar import. A member is not required to maintain a separate trust account for each client. No funds belonging to the member or the law firm shall be deposited therein or otherwise commingled therewith except as follows:

(1) Funds reasonably sufficient to pay bank charges.

(2) In the case of funds belonging in part to a client and in part presently or potentially to the member or the law firm, the portion belonging to the member or law firm must be withdrawn at the earliest reasonable time after the member's interest in that portion becomes fixed. However, when the right of the member or law firm to receive a portion of trust funds is disputed by the client, the disputed portion shall not be withdrawn until the dispute is finally resolved.

(B) A member shall:

* * * * *

(3) Maintain complete records of all funds, securities, and other properties of a client coming into the possession of the member or law firm and render appropriate accounts to the client regarding them.

(4) Promptly pay or deliver, as requested by the client, any funds, securities, or other properties in the possession of the member which the client is entitled to receive.

Paul Palomo v. State Bar of Columbia

Columbia Supreme Court (2004)

Paul Palomo was admitted to practice law in 1984. He has one instance of prior discipline. Here, the Hearing Department of the State Bar Court sustained allegations that Palomo willfully violated his oath and duties as an attorney and committed acts of dishonesty and moral turpitude when he (1) deposited the proceeds in his payroll account rather than his trust account, (2) failed promptly to notify the client he had received the check and to pay over the funds due. We uphold the findings of fact and adopt the disciplinary recommendation.

In December 2000, Jose Antonio Torres retained Ronald Roman, a member of Palomo's law firm, to represent Torres in connection with the New York probate of his father's estate. Torres paid a retainer fee of $75 and signed a retainer agreement. Roman left Palomo's employ around March 2001. On April 20th, Palomo's firm received a partial distribution check for $3,000 from the estate's representatives. The check was mistakenly deposited in the firm's *payroll* account. Five months later, after several inquiries from Torres, Palomo sent Torres a *trust* account check for $3,150, representing the earlier distribution plus "interest."

Palomo concedes his office mishandled the Torres check, but he disputes the finding of willful violations of an attorney's oath or duties. As he notes, his unrebutted testimony placed the blame on human error by an employee of his firm. Thus, he urges, while the record may show his negligence, it does not demonstrate intentional misconduct or dishonesty.

Palomo testified he told his office manager, Ms. M, to deposit the Torres check in the trust account; she mistakenly placed it in the payroll account instead. According to Palomo, Ms. M had complete banking and bookkeeping control; she could draw checks on the payroll account without his specific approval by using a stamp bearing his signature. Ms. M had previously handled client, operations, and payroll accounts for a major law firm. He also contends that he met with his accountant monthly to review the status of office accounts.

However, Palomo acknowledged that he gave Ms. M no supervision, *never* instructed her on trust account requirements and procedures, and *never* examined either her records or the bank statements for any of the office accounts. In any event, Palomo's office administration permitted the fact that a substantial client check endorsed by him had been misdeposited, commingled, and misappropriated to escape his notice for four months. There is no indication the error would ever have been discovered but for outside inquiry. Any procedure so lax as to produce that result was grossly negligent.

Palomo's contention overlooks the fact that attorneys assume a personal obligation of reasonable care to comply with the critically important rules for the safekeeping and disposition of client funds. Attorneys cannot be held responsible for every detail of office operations. However, where fiduciary violations occur as the result of serious and inexcusable lapses in office procedure, they may be deemed "willful" for disciplinary purposes, even if there was no deliberate wrongdoing. Indeed, mere evidence that the balance in a trust account fell below the amount credited to a client has been said to support a finding of willful misappropriation.

We have repeatedly held that trust account deficiencies are attributable to attorneys, not to their employees. Some decisions imply that only "gross" negligence or "habitual" disregard of client interests warrants discipline, but the record demonstrates such pervasive carelessness here.

Palomo's own testimony thus describes a pattern of gross negligence involving serious violations of an attorney's duty to oversee client funds entrusted to his care, and to keep detailed records and accounts thereof. These omissions resulted in a four-month delay in notifying the client that money due him had arrived, and in transmitting the funds promptly due. In the meantime, the funds were converted to the use of Palomo's office. There is no indication that Palomo would have remedied the irregularities if not pressed by the interested parties.[1]

Discipline

We conclude that Palomo's conduct warrants at least the lenient discipline recommended by the State Bar Court.

Affirmed.

---

[1] Petitioner points out that, when advised of his oversight, he promptly remitted the funds with "interest." While this fact may weigh in mitigation of discipline, it does not detract from the finding of willful violation.

Butts v. State Bar

Columbia Supreme Court (1977)

The State Bar charged Leonard Butts with three acts of professional misconduct, amounting to moral turpitude and dishonesty, all committed in connection with his employment as an attorney by his client Janette Mack.

The Review Department concluded that Butts should be subjected to discipline for only one of the acts charged, that of wrongfully withholding $253, and recommended that Butts be suspended from practice for a period of three months.

Butts was admitted to practice in 1971. About January, 1976, Robert Mack and his wife Janette separated and the husband commenced an action for divorce in Angeles County. Janette employed Butts to represent her in the matter. A property settlement agreement was executed by the spouses. This agreement provided for the payment to Janette of $1,000, effected by having Robert deliver the $1,000 to Butts for deposit in his trustee account. Butts was to hold the funds, subject to the fulfillment of the condition that Janette secure a decree of divorce in Nevada before November 1, 1976, but that in the event that Janette failed to deliver to Robert the decree of divorce, the $1,000 was to be returned to Robert Mack.

Janette went to Nevada to establish a residence for divorce, but before she had completed her compliance with the residence requirements in that state, she returned to Columbia, retained a new attorney, and instituted a divorce action in Angeles County.

On October 30th, Butts wrote Janette's new attorney and Robert's attorney, telling them: "I consider myself to be purely an escrow holder and, not wishing to become personally liable to either party, I must refuse to disburse the fund in my hands until such time as the parties jointly agree upon the disposition. If no such joint agreement is reached, I shall interplead in the pending divorce action and pay the money into Court."

On November 9th Janette died, and on November 11th Butts again wrote the attorney for Robert, saying: "By reason of her death I am apparently required to return to you the monies I hold under my trust receipt. I advanced to Janette Mack, from my personal funds, $200 for her living expenses since she had no personal funds with which to subsist. In addition to this advance there were other small advances, either to her or on account of court costs in the actions I handled for her, aggregating $53. For convenience, I have deducted these amounts from the sum I held. If this arrangement is not satisfactory to you, please inform me and I will send my check for the deductions and seek other means of collection." After the writing of this letter, Butts drew checks on the $1,000 fund, reimbursing himself in the sum of $253 and making the balance of $747 payable to Mr. Mack. Mr. Mack refused to accept the latter sum in full satisfaction of Butts's obligation and demanded an additional $253, which Butts paid promptly.

Butts contends that he practiced no deceit or dishonesty upon anyone; that the $253 represented amounts that he had advanced to the wife for necessaries, for which he thought he could hold the husband liable. Moreover, he thought that the wife's estate too would be liable for his claim. Further, Butts contends that the property settlement agreement was invalid because it was promotive of divorce and contrary to public policy.

The several legal points involving the validity of the challenged provision need not be determined; for purposes of this opinion the provision may be assumed to be valid. While Butts is in a doubtful position to claim exoneration upon the ground of an invalidity, his conduct should be appraised in the light of the situation as it presented itself to him at the time the alleged wrongful acts were committed.

The undisputed facts show that the error committed by Butts was not so much one of professional misconduct as one of failure to correctly assess his legal rights upon the death of the wife. That is, Butts in effect sought, by retaining the $253, to compel an accounting between the husband and the wife's estate. However, he was in possession of the $253 in a fiduciary and not a personal capacity, and therefore was not entitled to withhold it to offset a personal claim.

However, in view of the unusual circumstances and the complex legal problems inherent in the situation, the mistake appears to have been one of poor judgment as to the law and the proper procedure to protect his rights. To hold that it involved moral turpitude or constituted an act of professional misconduct would not be justified. He had acted openly and in good faith in asserting a valid claim for $253. He erred only in his attempted method of collection.

Further, we accept Butts's argument that he was legally obligated to keep the funds in trust when faced with the competing demands. Arguably, Butts was not obligated to pay the fund to either Janette's estate or Robert, since both sides claimed the funds. An attorney who receives money on behalf of a party who is not the attorney's client becomes a fiduciary to the party. When an attorney assumes the responsibility to disburse funds as agreed by the parties in an action, the attorney owes an obligation to the party who is not the attorney's client to ensure compliance with the terms of the agreement.

We conclude that there was no violation and that the discipline recommended should not have been imposed.

In the Matter of Jon Michael, A Member of the State Bar

Review Department of the State Bar Court (2009)

Jon Michael was admitted to practice law in 1993 and has no prior record of discipline. He was the sole attorney in a high-volume personal injury litigation practice in Central Valley for eleven years, and the firm grew to eight employees at its peak. In 1999 and again in 2003, Michael suffered significant back injuries. Michael's injuries and subsequent divorce left him in a depressed state. He also complained about his lack of desire, pain from his injuries, loss of energy due to Graves' disease (which was diagnosed around that time), emotional isolation and the need to be closer to his parents. Michael stopped coming to work regularly, and at the end of December 2004, he shut down his office, moved to southern Columbia, and filed for bankruptcy.

When he closed his office, Michael opened a post office box in Cerritos in December 2004, but did not update his State Bar membership records address until May 2005.

The disciplinary charges stem from Michael's handling of settlement funds on behalf of Kara Hughes, who hired him in 2002 to represent her after she was injured in an automobile accident. When the case settled in March 2004, State Farm Insurance (State Farm) sent Michael a check for $10,000, which he deposited in his client trust account (CTA). Shortly thereafter, Hughes went to Michael's office and he provided her with a settlement breakdown statement as follows: $5,405 to Hughes; $3,000 for attorney fees and $915 for costs to Michael; and the remaining $680 to reimburse Blue Cross Insurance Company (Blue Cross) for medical costs it paid on behalf of Hughes in 2003. Michael gave Hughes a check for her portion of the funds, which she promptly cashed.

On July 20, 2004, Michael wrote a CTA check for $680 to Blue Cross. Although Michael's standard office procedure was to have his office manager mail settlement checks, there is no evidence that the check was mailed or that Blue Cross received it. The check was not debited from the CTA.

Michael failed to realize that the check never cleared the bank because he did not have an adequate method of reconciling his CTA. Michael used a simple system for reconciling the CTA by comparing check withdrawals listed on monthly bank statements to check stubs in his checkbook. He did not review the stubs to ensure that all checks had cleared. He did not reconcile the monthly balance in his CTA with his bank statement.

When Michael closed his office in December of 2004, he did not close his CTA or reconcile the remaining balance in the account at the time. On February 15, 2005, the CTA balance dropped to $312, where it remained until at least 2007. This amount was $368 less than the $680 of Hughes's remaining settlement funds owed to Blue Cross that should have been kept in the CTA. In late 2005, Hughes received notice from Blue Cross that it had not been reimbursed for her medical expenses. She attempted to contact Michael, but found his office closed and his telephone disconnected. Hughes filed a complaint with the State Bar and an investigator sent letters to Michael, but Michael rarely checked mail due to his pain and had delegated the responsibility of picking up his mail to his cousin, who was unreliable and prone to misplacing the mail. Michael did not receive the State Bar letters.

State Bar Deputy Trial Counsel eventually located Michael and informed him of the investigation. Michael then sent Hughes a personal check for $680 within a week.

The State Bar served the formal notice of disciplinary charges (NDC) on Michael charging him with four counts of misconduct

After a two-day contested disciplinary hearing, involving the four counts of misconduct in one client matter, the hearing judge found Michael culpable of a single trust account violation and recommended that he receive a one-year stayed suspension and a two-year period of probation with no period of actual suspension. The Chief Trial Counsel of the State Bar sought review, contending that Michael should be found culpable of three additional counts of misconduct, including misappropriation, and that the recommended discipline should be increased to include an actual suspension of one year. We adopt the hearing judge's finding of culpability but also find Michael culpable of misappropriation, failing to promptly return client funds and failing to cooperate with a State Bar investigation. In light of the additional culpability, as well as aggravating factors, we recommend a 90-day actual suspension as a condition of a one-year stayed suspension and a two-year period of probation.

Count One (Rule 4-100(A))

We agree with the hearing judge's finding that Michael failed to maintain client funds in his trust account in willful violation of Rule 4-100(A) because the balance fell below the $680 required to be held in trust for Hughes. An attorney entrusted with client funds "assume[s] a personal obligation of reasonable care to comply with the critically important rules for the safekeeping and disposition of client funds." (*Palomo v. State Bar* (2004).) This duty requires an attorney to maintain client funds in the CTA until outstanding balances are settled. Although it may not be deliberate, a trust account violation caused by "serious and inexcusable lapses in office procedure" is "willful" for disciplinary purposes. (*Palomo v. State Bar, supra.*) There is clear and convincing evidence that Michael willfully violated Rule 4-100(A) by not maintaining the balance of Hughes's settlement funds in his CTA.

It is well-established that, even if an attorney's conduct is unintentional, carelessness leading to trust account violations may involve moral turpitude. We find that Michael's gross negligence in handling his CTA, and the resulting misappropriation, constitute a willful violation of the rules. (*Palomo v. State Bar, supra.*)

Michael failed to properly manage his CTA. Michael failed to implement or follow the most basic procedures to safeguard his CTA. From October 2003 until he closed his office in December 2004, Michael did not even attempt to reconcile the monthly balance in his CTA. His carelessness and gross negligence resulted in the misappropriation of $368 of Hughes's settlement funds and constitutes conduct amounting to moral turpitude.

Count Two (Rule 4-100(B)(4))

We also find Michael culpable of violating Rule 4-100(B)(4). This rule requires an attorney to promptly pay funds to which the client is entitled, and extends to third parties to whom the attorney has agreed to distribute the client funds. Michael had notice of Blue Cross's medical lien and requests for payment. Michael testified that he negotiated a reduction in the amount owed and agreed to pay Blue Cross on behalf of Hughes. Further, as is evident from the settlement breakdown statement, Hughes anticipated that Michael would use the remaining funds to reimburse Blue Cross. Michael failed to satisfy his obligation to reimburse Blue Cross on behalf of Hughes as promised, in willful violation of Rule 4-100(B)(4).

Count Three (Section 6068)

The final count alleges that Michael failed to cooperate with the State Bar during its investigation, in violation of Section 6068. The hearing judge found that Michael was not culpable because Michael did not receive the letters the State Bar sent in December 2005 and January 2006, and then he fully cooperated once he was located in February 2007. We do not agree.

After Michael closed his practice in December 2004, he decided to "drop from the face of the earth." Michael failed to update his State Bar membership record address until five months later. Even after updating his State Bar records, for over a year he depended on his cousin, whom he knew to be unreliable, to check his mailbox. Michael's own gross carelessness in fulfilling his ethical duties prevented the State Bar from contacting him for over a year. Michael's carelessness showed indifference to his obligations to his former clients and to the State Bar, frustrated the investigation of this matter, and thus, constitutes a willful violation of Section 6068. To hold otherwise would only condone an attorney's ostrich-like behavior, which we are unwilling to do.

DISCIPLINE

The primary purposes of disciplinary proceedings are the protection of the public and the courts and the legal profession, the maintenance of high professional standards for attorneys, and the preservation of public confidence in the legal profession. There is no fixed formula for determining the proper level of discipline.

We do not find that Michael acted pursuant to a good faith belief that he had paid Blue Cross because this assumption was unreasonable in light of his inadequate accounting procedures. When Michael closed his office, the balance remaining in his CTA clearly should have alerted him to a problem requiring investigation. His decision to do nothing was unreasonable.

For all the reasons cited, we recommend that Jon Michael be suspended for one year, that execution of that suspension be stayed, and that he be placed on probation for two years on the conditions that he must be suspended from the practice of law for the first 90 days of probation.

In the Matter of Stephine Webb, A Member of the State Bar

Review Department of the State Bar Court (2006)

In this proceeding, the Office of the Chief Trial Counsel of the State Bar seeks disbarment for Stephine Webb's alleged commingling of client trust funds with personal funds, and her failure to cooperate with the State Bar.

Webb was admitted to the practice of law in 1984. Webb had been married, but is now divorced. As a result of the divorce, Webb obtained a post office box in San Fe, Columbia to be used as her official membership records address, so that her ex-husband could not track her down. Because this mailbox was used for such a limited purpose, she often did not check it.

In November 2004, Webb was diagnosed with breast cancer. She had surgery to remove the tumor in December 2004 and chemotherapy and radiation for her cancer. During the period, she felt very fatigued and uncomfortable, and was unable to attend to her regular duties at work. In fact, she only worked a couple days in the month.

Count One: Commingling Personal Funds in CTA

Rule 4-100(A) provides that all funds received for the benefit of clients must be deposited in a client trust account (CTA) and that no funds belonging to the attorney shall be deposited therein or otherwise commingled therewith.

The State Bar investigator reviewed the bank statements of the CTA. He identified several deposits that made him feel that Webb was commingling her own funds with those in the CTA. The State Bar attorneys simply adopted his numbers and inserted them in the notice of disciplinary charges, and then offered no other proof that the deposits and withdrawals were improper.

At trial, Webb satisfactorily explained the deposits and withdrawals identified by the investigator. The State Bar has therefore failed to sustain its burden of proof by clear and convincing evidence as to the commingling alleged in Count One.

Count Two: Failure to Cooperate in State Bar Investigation

Section 6068 provides that an attorney must cooperate and participate in any disciplinary investigation or proceeding pending against the attorney.

The State Bar investigator sent Webb a letter requesting a written response, dated February 25, 2005, addressed to Webb at her official membership records address. The letter was not returned by the post office, nor was it responded to by Webb. On March 18, 2005, the investigator sent a second letter to Webb's official membership records address requesting the same information. This letter was also not returned by the post office, nor was it responded to by Webb.

On April 21, 2005, the investigator spoke with William Hopkins, the named partner in Webb's firm, who is also Webb's son. Also on the same day, the investigator spoke with Webb. He learned from Webb that she was ill with cancer, and that because of her illness, she was not checking her post office box for mail. She told him that she would soon respond to his two letters. However, he never received anything from Webb.

On June 9, 2005, Webb changed her official membership records address to a post office box in Tiburon, Columbia. On October 13, 2005, the investigator sent Webb a letter to her new official membership records address. This letter was not returned by the post office, nor was it responded to by Webb. As before, a follow-up letter was sent to Webb's official membership records address requesting the same information. Again, the letter was not returned by the post office as undeliverable, nor was it responded to by Webb.

The charge of failing to cooperate with the State Bar in willful violation of Section 6068 is based solely on the failure to respond to these notices. Alone, that would establish a prima facie case of violation of Section 6068.

Webb's failure to cooperate with the State Bar was either in the middle of her chemotherapy and radiation treatment for cancer, or during her recovery, albeit near the end. During the entire period from her initial surgery through

November 2005, however, Webb credibly testified that she suffered from serious fatigue and an inability to focus on managing her business. Further, the State Bar investigator was aware of her medical condition. It is significant to note that when she was contacted prior to her diagnosis and commencement of treatment, she cooperated fully. Her timely correspondence with the State Bar only stopped when she received the bad news of her cancer and began her treatment.

As such, the court finds that, at least with respect to the alleged violation of Section 6068, compelling mitigating circumstances existed which clearly predominated. The State Bar has also failed to sustain its burden of proof by clear and convincing evidence as to the commingling alleged in Count One.

The charges therefore are dismissed with prejudice.

PT-A: SELECTED ANSWER 1

TO: Chief Trial Counsel
FROM: Applicant
Date: February 23, 2016
SUBJECT: In the Matter of Milly Nolan Fleck

I have analyzed each of the four charges (2 charges under Rule 4-100(A), one charge under Rule 4-100(B), and one charge under section 6068). Below please find my summary of the law applicable to each of these sections and the application to Fleck's circumstances. In my analysis, I presented a more neutral view under the best light possible from a prosecutor's perspective. As a prosecutor, I have the duty to ensure that justice be done. I am duty bound <u>not</u> to pursue a conviction at all costs.

Executive Summary

1. Rule 4-100(A) - Failure to Maintain Appropriate Funds in CTA

Under Rule 4-100(A), Fleck's CTA was in a shortage of $10 for about six weeks. This shortage resulted in a $490 CTA balance when, in fact, Fleck should still have $500 in the CTA (an amount owing to Hersh, as discussed in 4-100(B)). Fleck's procedures were not adequate to prevent such shortages from occurring and should be appropriately disciplined. Although the amount of shortage and length of time is minimal, this should not be encouraged.

2. Rule 4-100(B) - Failure to Promptly Pay Funds to Client

The State Bar will **likely prevail** against Fleck for violating Rule 4-100(B) by not paying the client the $500 in client funds when requested by the client. The evidence suggests that the lawyer's decision not to pay the client was deliberate in order to extract an unrelated promise from the client. The lawyer's conduct should not be encouraged.

3. Rule 4-100(A) - Commingling her own funds in CTA

Under this Rule, the State Bar is **unlikely to prevail** on a charge against Fleck for violating Rule 4-100(A) for depositing $125 of her own funds into the account. Fleck likely falls within the exception provided under Rule 4-100(A)(2).

4. Section 6068 - Failure to Cooperate

Under this Section, the State Bar appears to have **two complaints**. First, Fleck did <u>not</u> update her mailing address for a few months. Second, Fleck did not attend the physical interview when requested by the investigator. As discussed below, the State Bar will likely prevail on a charge against Fleck for violating Section 6068 for not maintaining the mailing address or responding to the State Bar notices.

However, on the second complaint, the failure to attend a physical interview, the State Bar will **likely not prevail** on a charge against Fleck for violating Section 6068.

5. Recommended Sanction/Penalty

It appears from the case law that the disciplinary measures depends on the lawyer's past history of disciplinary actions and how serious the violations were.

There is no fixed formula. The key is that the Court must maintain the public confidence in the legal profession and maintenance of high professional standards. The violations here are comparable to those in *Michael*.

The most serious violation here is that Fleck intentionally violated Rule 4-100(B), whereas in *Michael* the violation of 4-100(B) was less serious. However, in *Michael* the violation of section 6068 appeared to be very serious and amounted to gross negligence. Whereas, Fleck's violation of Section 6068 is not as serious. Finally, Fleck's violation of Rule 4-100(A), both in terms of dollar amount and length of time, is nowhere comparable to the violation in *Michael*. Furthermore, Fleck's procedures for reconciling the CTA is not up to standard, but certainly not to the very poor level in *Michael*.

Overall, the sanctions provided in *Michael* would be a good <u>general</u> guidance for the State Bar in recommending a disciplinary measure for Fleck. In *Michael*, the lawyer was suspended for 1 year and placed on probation for two years (with the first 90 days of probation a suspension from the practice of law). There is no information on Fleck's past disciplinary history. Assuming this was Fleck's first disciplinary action, considering she has six years of practice experience, she is not considered very senior. The appropriate sanctions should be less than *Michael* with a specific length of suspension given the seriousness of the Rule 4-100(B) violation.

Applicable Laws

Rule 4-100(A) - Columbia Rules of Professional Conduct (the "Rules")

Under this Rule 4-100(A), we can dissect two duties that the lawyer must fulfill as part of his ethical obligations.

Firstly, the lawyer has a duty to maintain appropriate funds in his/her Client Trust Account (the "CTA"). For example, if the lawyer, in the aggregate, has received $5,000 in trust from clients, his CTA should have no less than $5,000.

Secondly, the lawyer has a duty not to commingle his/her own funds with the trust funds in the CTA. However, there some express exceptions under paragraph (1) and (2) of this Rule. Generally, the lawyer is permitted to deposit his/her own funds for purposes of reasonably satisfying the bank charges. The lawyer shall also maintain funds in the CTA if the ownership of the funds is being disputed. That is, if the client is disputing whether the lawyer is entitled to those funds or whether the client is entitled to them, the lawyer must maintain that portion of the money in the CTA until the matter is finally resolved. Thereafter, the lawyer must withdraw the money at his/her easliest reasonable time.

Burden of Proof under Rule 4-100(A)

From the case law, we see that the burden of proof for a finding a violation under this rule is that the prosecution must provide **clear and convincing evidence** (*In the Matter of Stephine Webb,* [*Webb*]). The *Webb* case and the *Matter of Jon Michael* [*Michael*] case both applied the **clear and convincing standard** to a finding relating to maintaining appropriate funds in the lawyer's CTA. The cases did not discuss the burden of proof for finding a violating that the lawyer has commingled his/her own funds with the client's funds in the CTA. However, it is likely that the same burden of proof (i.e. **clear and convincing evidence**) should also apply to a violating relating to commingling of funds. Both violations are under Rule 4-100(A) and it would be illogical to have different burdens of proof within the same Rule.

Actus Reas and Mens Rea under Rule 4-100(A)

The prosecution must show, using clear and convincing evidence, that the lawyer engaged in the **act** and had the requisite **intent**. The act in relation to both commingling of client funds with the lawyer's funds and duty to maintain appropriate funds in the trust account can be satisfied through reviewing the accounting records. Most of the time, it would be clear whether or not the lawyer has committed the **act**. The cases that I have reviewed focused on whether the lawyer had the requisite intent to find a violation of the Rule. It is clear from the case that the lawyer is not held to a strict liability standard. There must be *some* intent by the lawyer when he committed the violation of the Rule, no matter how minimal the intent or whether the intent is inferred from surrounding circumstances.

In *Paul v Palomo*, it is suggested that some cases imply that only **gross negligence** or **habitual disregard** would warrant discipline under this Rule. In *Michael* citing *Palomo*, the Review Board found that a trust account violation caused by "serious and inexcusable lapses in office procedure" is willful for disciplinary purposes. It does <u>not</u> matter that the lawyer's conduct was not intentional; even carelessness would warrant disciplinary action under this Rule. A failure to implement or follow the most basic procedures to safeguard the CTA has been found to be a violation of the Rule. In *Michael,* the lawyer was found in violation of the rule when he failed to reconcile his CTA for about 14 months.

In *Palomo*, the Supreme Court went as far as stating that <u>mere evidence</u> that the balance of a trust account falling below the amount credited to a client has been said to support a finding of willful misappropriation. It is important to note that the lawyer has a duty to properly supervise and instruct any staff members that deal with the CTA. It is the lawyer's own obligation that can be simply delegated and forgotten about.

Application of Rule 4-100(A) to the Facts in Present Case - Commingling Her Own Funds in the CTA

One allegation by the State Bar is that Fleck deposited $125 of her own personal funds into the CTA and thereby commingled the funds contrary to Rule 4-100(A). As discussed above, the burden of proof is **clear and convincing evidence**. However, Fleck has provided a reasonable explanation for why the funds were deposited into the CTA in the first place. The lawyer explained that the $125 was intended for checks and a leather ledger. It is likely not for the State Bar to determine whether the lawyer should or should not buy a leather ledger. Considering the surrounding circumstances and the high costs of banking in recent years, it is **not unreasonable** to conclude that $125 is a reasonbly sufficient amount to pay bank charges. As a result, Fleck would likely be able to invoke the exception under Rule 4-100(A)(1). A charge of an ethical violation in relation to the $125 in personal funds is **unlikely to succeed**.

Application of Rule 4-100(A) to the Facts in Present Case - Failure to Maintain Appropriate Funds in the CTA

Another allegation by the State Bar is that Fleck failed to maintain appropriate funds in the CTA. It appears that the two transactions are key to this violation:

- the $500 supposedly held for Ms. Hersh in trust

- On February 18, 2015 receiving two checks, each for $250 from a Client A. The lawyer (through his assistant) deposited one check to the general account and one to the trust account. Then on March 19, 2015, the lawyer issued a trust check for $385 (which is greater than the amount held in trust from this client).

- Even if we assume that the $125 from the lawyer can be considered trust funds with the CTA, the lawyer is still short $10 in her trust account from March 27, 2015 to April 30, 2015, about six weeks.

- From the facts, we see that Fleck kept her own ledger of the CTA and did not delegate this responsibility. The lawyer also reconciled the ledger with the bank records periodically, at least annually. It would appear that an **annual** reconciliation is too long. Trust accounts should, as a matter of general practice, be reconciled at least more regularly (i.e. monthly).

- In addition, with respect to the funds from Client A, at the time the lawyer received the checks, the lawyer should have deposited them both into the CTA. However, as discussed above, the lawyer is likely not held to a standard of strict liability. Given the surrounding circumstances, it was quite reasonable for Fleck (and the assistant, Mr. Gold) to infer that one check should be meant for trust and one check for the general account. After all, it makes no logical sense for the client to make two checks out to the same account (assuming both checks were written from the same bank account). Thus, it is **unlikely** for the State Bar to find that the lawyer violated Rule 4-100(A) with respect to the depositing of Client A's checks into her own general account.

- However, the issuing of a trust check for $385 from the CTA when the amount of funds for Client A is only $250 would appear to be a *prima facie* violation of Rule 4-100(A). The lawyer would instantly recognize this if she checked her ledger prior to issuing a trust check. Unfortunately, it appears that this verification was not part of the standard procedures. It should be part of the standard procedure for the lawyer to cross-check before issuing a trust check to the client. It is **likely** for the State Bar to succeed in a case for violation of Rule 4-100(A) when the lawyer issued the $385 check. Though the State Bar would succeed in finding a violation of Rule 4-100(A), the sanctions in relation to this particular act should not be severe. This is mainly because the amount of time when the CTA was in a shortage was not long (i.e. about six weeks) and the amount in question was low (i.e. $10).

Rule 4-100(B)

Under this Rule, the lawyer must maintain complete records of client's funds/securities/properties in the lawyer's possession (sub (3)). The lawyer must also promptly pay or deliver the funds to the client, for which the client is entitled to (sub(4)). The remaining analysis below will focus on Rule 4-100(B)(4).

According to *Butts v State Bar*, the lawyer is not held to a strict liability standard. It appears that the lawyer may withhold client funds if the lawyer makes a reasonable mistake as to whether the lawyer is entitled to hold such funds to offset debts owed to that lawyer by the client. Although in *Butts*, it is clear that a lawyer who receives money on behalf of a party who is not the lawyer's client becomes a fiduciary of that party, the lawyer is entitled to make reasonable mistakes as to who has the legal right to the money. In *Butts*, the lawyer was found <u>not</u> to be in violation due to a reasonable mistake.

On the other hand, we see in *Michael* that Rule 4-100(B)(4) ought to be read **broadly** so as to confer the protection not only to the client, but also to third parties whom the lawyer has agreed to distribute the client funds. In *Michael*, the lawyer was in violation of this Rule when he did not have an adequate method of reconciling the CTA and thus did not realize the issue until prompted by the third party. From the facts, it was unclear who made the error (whether it was the law firm staff or even the post office). The lawyer insisted that he disbursed a check to the third party, but there was no record of mailing or receipt. It appears that the test used by the Court is "whether the lawyer has appropriate measures for avoiding such scenarios <u>and</u> whether the lawyer in fact followed such procedures".

The cases do not cover whether the standard is **clear and convincing evidence** or **balance of probabilities**. In any case, it is more likely that the standard should be **clear and convincing evidence** so that there is uniformity within the ethical rules. In any event, I will discuss both standards of proof in my application of Rule 4-100(B) to the facts.

Application of Rule 4-100(B) to the Facts in Present Case

The issue in question is whether Fleck failed to **promptly pay the $500** to Hersh. As a starting point, before going into Rule 4-100(B), we need to establish whether the ownership of the funds is the client's or the lawyer's. If the $500 was a **true retainer fee** under Rule 3-700 (D)(2), then the $500 is clearly Fleck's money and there could be no finding of violation under Rule 4-100(B)(4). At most, there **may** be a violation of Rule 4-100(A)(2) for not withdrawing the money at the earliest reasonable time.

A **true retainer fee** is an amount to secure the lawyer's availability and is earned when paid.

From the facts, it appears that the $500 is more likely to be an advance of future fees, and not a **true retainer fee**. In Hersh's interview, she stated that Fleck wanted a "retainer of $500 <u>as an advance</u>". In Fleck's correspondence with Hersh, she also referred to the $500 as "for future work on the child custody matter". As such, the $500 is not exempted under Rule 3-700(D)(2) and we must look into Rule 4-100(B).

In Fleck's case, it does not involve payment to a third party. The $500 was, supposedly, to be paid to the client. Rule 4-100(B)(4) *prima facie* applies and the lawyer must promptly pay/deliver the funds to the client.

In the facts, Fleck offered to return the $500 retainer if Hersh signed a substitution of lawyers form. Hersh signed that form and returned it to Fleck for cross-signature. However, Fleck returned the signed form but not the $500. Hersh **clearly requested** Fleck to return the $500 when the form was returned.

Fleck failed to return the money. There appears to be no dispute that the $500 is the client's money and the client also **requested** its return. This falls squarely into Rule 4-100(B)(4). Fleck is in clear violation of this Rule.

Fleck's excuse for keeping the $500 was because Hersh did not **properly** execute the release for the personal injury file. Given the facts, there was no indication that Hersh was disputing the validity of the settlement in the personal injury file. In any event, if there was a dispute, the Court would likely find that Hersh accepted the settlement by conduct (e.g. cashing the check) and Hersh would have unclean hands if she were to challenge the settlement for the personal injury file.

While the case law says that a reasonable mistake as to the ownership of the funds or misunderstanding of the laws leading to an incorrect collection procedure would exonerate the lawyer under Rule 4-100(B)(4), this is **likely** not applicable in the present case. Fleck clearly admitted in the interview that the unsigned release for the PI file was **the only reason** that the $500 was not being returned. Fleck admitted that she kept the $500 to "encourage" the client to sign the release. This is clearly improper conduct. Put bluntly, this appears to be a case where the lawyer is holding the client's money ransom in exchange for something. Fleck did <u>not</u> make a reasonable mistake as to the ownership of this $500. Fleck was not exercising an "incorrect collection procedure" to secure funds that Fleck *believes* she owns. This is a clear blatant violation of Rule 4-100(B)(4) that is not exempted in *Butts*. Fleck's defense for holding the $500 to "encourage" the client to sign the release for the PI file cannot succeed.

The State Bar will **likely prevail** against Fleck for a violation under Rule 4-100(B)(4). Given the convincing evidence above, including Fleck's own admission at the interview (assuming the interview is admissible evidence), the State Bar will prevail against Fleck regardless if the burden was **balance of**

probabilities or **clear and convincing evidence**. There is clear and convincing evidence of a violation in Fleck's case.

Section 6068 - Columbia Professions Code (the "Code")

Under Section 6068 of the _Code_ all lawyers must cooperate and participate in any disciplinary investigation against himself or herself. Like the other Rules discussed above, the lawyer is not held to a strict liability standard. It appears that the Court (or Review Panel) would view this from a case-by-case basis.

In _Michael_, the Court found that a violation of section 6068 can be found based on failure to update State Bar membership address information for 5 months and relying on an unreliable person for over one year to collect the lawyer's mail at a mailbox. The court made this finding despite the lawyer fully cooperating after learning of the complaint 1 year and 2 months later.

However, in _In the Matter of Stephine Webb_, the Court stated, as a rule, that failure to respond to notices from the State Bar is a _prima facie_ violation of Section 6068. However, the Court also recognized compelling mitigating circumstances including: the lawyer was in medical treatment when the notices were received, the State Bar was fully aware of the lawyer's medical circumstances; and the lawyer was fully cooperating prior to obtaining the medical treatment. The Court also reiterated that the standard under Section 6068 is **clear and convincing evidence**.

From the above, we can dissect, as a general rule that failure to respond to State Bar notices is a violation of Section 6068 absent some compelling mitigating circumstances such as a medical condition. In addition, the lawyer must fully cooperate immediately after the medical condition ceases to exist.

Application to Fleck's Case

In Fleck's case, there are two series of facts that *may* be captured under section 6068. Firstly, her failure to respond to State Bar notices. Secondly, her "refusal" to attend a state bar interview in person.

In Fleck's case, State Bar notices were sent on June 28, 2015, July 20, 2015 and August 30, 2015. None of the notices were received by Fleck because Fleck closed her practice. Fleck's reason was that she needed to take a break with her mother for a couple of months after her father had died.

Only four months later did Fleck update her State Bar records and corresponded with the State Bar. Although Fleck's conduct in not updating her State Bar records is not as serious as in *Michael*, Fleck clearly had the opportunity to update the records or find someone to look after her mail while she was away attending to family duties. Fleck is **likely** in *prima facie* violation of Section 6068 for failure to update records. The Court, as in *Webb*, would consider mitigating circumstances. In the present case, Fleck's case for mitigating circumstances appear to be her father's death and having to spend time with her mother. This is clearly distinguishable from *Webb*.

In *Webb*, it was **the lawyer herself** that was affected by a medical condition and had to take a break from work and the office. In the present case, Fleck appears to be a fully healthy person and was only absent to tend to family matters. While the State Bar should be sympathetic to the lawyer's personal situation, the State Bar has a duty in maintaining a high standard for professional conduct. The State Bar cannot simply allow the lawyer to use "family duties" as a mitigating circumstance to excuse himself/herself from fulfilling the ethical duties. This is especially the case where the lawyer is **physically able** to arrange the affairs properly. Fleck cannot use the excuse of "too busy" or "family duties" as mitigating circumstances and the court should not accept it either. As a result, there is **very likely** a strong case of a Section 6068 by not updating State Bar records.

On the other hand, there is **likely no violation of Section 6068** when Fleck is reluctant to meet. In the interview, the investigator requested that Fleck "come into our office for a more extensive review". Fleck refused on the ground that she has too much work and too busy. Instead, Fleck offered to have Mr. Gold provide all the necessary information for the investigation and fully cooperate. From the Memorandum written by the investigator, it is clear that Mr. Gold is ready to fully cooperate and offered as much as he can. There was no subpoena for Fleck's attendance at the interview. Rule 6068 requires cooperation, not physical attendance. In addition, the investigator appears to have "waived" the physical attendance when she said "if you will not come in, then we will leave it there for the moment". There is no **clear and convincing evidence** that Fleck is refusing to cooperate with the State Bar. Practically speaking, there are times when a lawyer is too busy with his/her files. Unless there is clear evidence that the lawyer is refusing to cooperate, the Court is unlikely to find that the lawyer is in violation of Section 6068. If Fleck was issued a subpoena and still refused to attend, that will be a different story.

TO: Chief Trial Counsel
FROM: Applicant
DATE: February 23, 2016
SUBJECT: RE: In the Matter of Milly Nolan Fleck, Respondent

Dear Chief Trial Counsel,

I have received your memorandum regarding the matter of Milly Nolan Fleck. It is my understanding that claims arising from a Ms. Liora Hirsch that Ms. Fleck had misappropriated and withheld $500 from a personal injury settlement prompted an investigation into Ms. Fleck's negligent handling of her client trust account (CTA). The investigation uncovered facts which suggest Ms. Fleck may have commingled her own funds in her CTA, and that the balance in her CTA fell below the amount it should minimally have contained for a period of six weeks.

It is my understanding that the State Bar investigator has recommended that we charge Ms. Fleck with the following violations: (1) Rule 4-100(a) for failure to maintain appropriate funds in her CTA; (2) Rule 4-100(b) for failing to promptly pay funds to a client; (3) Rule 4-100(a) for commingling her own funds in her CTA; and (4) Section 6068 for failure to cooperate with a disciplinary investigation. You asked that I prepare a memorandum evaluating whether we can prevail on each of these charges. The following are my findings.

1. Rule 4-100(A): Failure to Maintain Appropriate Funds in her CTA

An attorney entrusted with client funds "assume[s] a personal obligation of reasonable care to comply with the critically important rules for the safekeeping and disposition of client funds." (PALOMO, JON MICHAEL). This duty requires an attorney to maintain client funds in the CTA until outstanding balances are settled. Although it may not be deliberate, a trust account violation caused by "serious and inexcusable lapses in office procedure" is "willful" for disciplinary purposes. (PALOMO, JON MICHAEL). The burden of proof is one of clear and convincing evidence that the respondent willfully violated Rule 4-100(A) by not maintaining appropriate funds in her CTA, and that burden is held by the State Bar

It is well-established that, even if an attorney's conduct is unintentional, carelessness leading to trust account violations may involve moral turpitude. (JON MICHAEL). A great illustration of this principle is Paul Palomo v. State Bar of Columbia. In this case, Palomo was found to have willfully violated his oath and duties as an attorney and to have committed acts of dishonesty and moral turpitude when he deposited proceeds from a probate into his payroll account rather than his client trust account. Palomo contended that he had an office manager who completed bookkeeping and all accounting, who had years of experience in office managing and that the misplacement of the check was simply a negligent mistake, but was not willful misconduct or dishonest. The court concluded otherwise. The court concluded that because Palomo gave his office manager no supervision, that because he never instructed her on trust account requirements and procedures, and because he never examined either her records or the bank statements for any of the office accounts, that his office procedures were so lax they constituted gross negligence on his part.

Here, Ms. Fleck's business practices began as the opposite those of Palomo's business practices in that she was very hands-on in her accounting practices. Ms. Fleck claims that she kept track of her client account with the help of Mr. Gold. Ms. Fleck claims that she signed any withdrawal, kept her own ledger of the CTA, and would reconcile her ledger with the bank records periodically, at least annually.

However, Ms. Fleck's accounting practices began to mirror those of Palomo's at the end of 2014 due to her father's illness. She claims that during this time while she was trying to care for her father and his business, she knew there were very few deposits and withdrawals from late 2014 until she closed the practice, and that she thought everything was in order. She neglected to maintain the prior practice of reconciling her ledger with her bank statements. If she had continued this practice, she would have realized that Mr. Gold had mistakenly deposited one of Client A's two advance checks for $250 into the practice's operating account. Though Mr. Gold was responsible for making deposits into the operating account, and Ms. Fleck did not have a history of inspecting the checks that went into the operating account, had she continued her good accounting practices into 2015, she would have realized much sooner that the balance in the CTA had dropped below the $500 she owed to Ms. Hersh. But she did not. In fact, very much like Jon Michael, she closed her practice in June 2015 and did not close her CTA or reconcile the remaining balance at the time of closure. Courts have repeatedly held that trust account deficiencies are attributable to attorneys, not their employees. (PALOMO). Thus, even though Mr. Gold was the one who misappropriated Client A's second advance into the operating account and not the client trust account, Ms. Fleck will remain liable as being grossly negligent.

Very much like Palomo, Ms. Fleck's own admissions through her telephone interview describe patterns of gross negligence involving serious violations of an attorney's duty to oversee client funds entrusted to her care, and to keep detailed records and accounts thereof. Just as in PALOMO, Mr. Gomez doubts that Ms. Fleck was aware of the misdeposit until the time he first spoke with her in October 2015, a full 7 months after the funds in the CTA dropped below the appropriate amount. He also believes that the inadequate funds would have stayed that way if it had not been brought to the attention of Ms. Fleck because she so negligently maintained, or rather failed to maintain the CTA funds.

For the foregoing reasons, the State Bar will be able to prevail on this charge against Ms. Fleck.

2. Rule 4-100(B): Failing to Promptly Pay Funds to a Client

Rule 4-100 (B)(4) requires an attorney to promptly pay funds to which the client is entitled, and extends to third parties to whom the attorney has agreed to distribute the client funds. (JON MICHAEL).

An attorney who receives money on behalf of a party who is not the attorney's client becomes a fiduciary to the party. When an attorney assumes the responsibility to disburse funds as agreed by the parties in an action, the attorney owes an obligation to the party who is not the attorney's client to ensure compliance with the terms of agreement. (BUTTS).

In BUTTS, the attorney acted correctly in keeping the money in his trust that was supposed to be paid to client once she satisfied a condition of payment, when she did not satisfy the condition.

Here, the $17,500 settlement was entrusted to Ms. Fleck as a fiduciary of the insurance company. As a term of the settlement agreement, per Ms. Fleck's letter to Ms. Hersh, Ms. Fleck was to provide the signed Release of All Claims to the insurance company as a condition of the settlement, and as a condition of signing the check for Ms. Hersh's recovery. According to the records, and to Ms. Fleck's testimony, Ms. Hersh never signed the Release form for the insurance company, even though Ms. Fleck made written requests to Hersh seven times, and sent her copies of the release in three of the requests. Thus, because the condition was never satisfied, the money was never supposed to be disbursed to Ms. Hersh. Ms. Fleck was in breach of her fiduciary duty to the insurance company because she allotted the funds to Ms. Hersh without complying with the terms set by the insurance company.

If the release had been signed, then the money would have been due to Ms. Hersh. Rule 3-700 provides that all money advanced to a professional should be returned to the client upon termination of the professional-client relationship. "True retainer fee[s]" which are paid solely for the purpose of ensuring the availability of the professional in the matter are exempt from this provision. However, an advance against future fees is not a retainer. Thus, it was correct for Fleck to keep the $500 until she was terminated from employment by Hersh.

However, because the release was never signed, the money was never due to Ms. Hersh; therefore, the State Bar will not prevail on the charge against Ms. Fleck for failure to promptly distribute client funds.

3. Rule 4-100(A): Commingling her own Funds in her CTA

Rule 4-100(A) provides that all funds received for the benefit of clients must be deposited in a client trust account (CTA) and that no funds belonging to the attorney shall be deposited therein or otherwise commingled therewith. The State Bar has the burden of proof by clear and convincing evidence as to the commingling alleged against the respondent. (WEBB). However, Rule 4-100(A)(1) also provides that funds belonging to a member or law firm may be commingled for the purpose of paying bank charges.

Here, Ms. Fleck has admitted that when she opened the new CTA in late 2014, she added about $125 for the purpose of buying new checks and a new check ledger. She anticipated the checks would cost approximately $100 and she wanted to buy a new leather ledger; thus she concluded $125 was a sufficient amount of funds to cover the cost. I am unsure whether the payment for a book of checks and a new ledger would be allowed to be categorized as "bank charges" for the purposes of Rule 4-100(A)(1). If so, then the State Bar has no charge against Ms. Fleck for a violation of Rule 4-100(A) as funds belonging to a member or law firm may be deposited and commingled in a CTA for the purpose of paying bank charges. However, if the payment of a book of checks and a check ledger do not constitute "bank charges", then the State Bar may establish that Ms. Fleck commingled her own personal funds with those in the CTA. Unlike in WEBB, where the State Bar investigator simply identified several deposits that made him feel like Webb had been commingling her funds in the CTA, Mr. Gomez can prove with clear and convincing evidence that Ms. Fleck was indeed commingling her funds with those in the CTA as he has procured her own admission and composed a reconciliation of the bank records.

Therefore, if payment for a book of checks and a check ledger constitute "bank charges" under Rule 4-100(A)(1), then the State Bar has no claim against Ms. Fleck. However, if they do not constitute "bank charges" for the purposes of Rule 4-100(A)(1), then the State Bar will be able to prevail on this charge.

4. Section 6068: Failure to Cooperate with a Disciplinary Investigation

Section 6068 provides that an attorney must cooperate and participate in any disciplinary investigation or proceeding pending against the attorney. Failure to respond to notices from the State Bar would establish a prima facie case of willful violation of Section 6068. A charge of a violation of Section 6068 can be mitigated if compelling circumstances existed at the time the investigation was being completed. (WEBB).

Here, Ms. Fleck's behavior mirrors that displayed by Jon Michael. She closed her practice in June of 2015, and had her mail forwarded to a mailbox. The State Bar sent her three notices which she did not respond to each in June, July, and August. Her failure to respond alone would create a prima facie case of willingly violating Section 6068 in her failure to cooperate with the investigation. She uses the excuse that she never received these notices even though she claims to have picked up the mail from every week or so, but that these notices must have been mailed when she was not checking the mailbox often. Like Jon Michael, she then dropped off the face of the earth in order to spend a couple of months with her mother. It was not until four months later (Jon Michael waited a full five months) that she finally updated her address with the State Bar. When the State Bar was finally able to get a hold of her, she continues to refuse to come into the office for questioning for no good reason. Unlike Ms. Webb who was able to use the crippling side effects of cancer as a mitigating circumstance, Ms. Fleck can show no mitigating compelling circumstances as she never was and currently is not sick, and has made no viable excuse to not show up in person to assist the investigators in the matter against her. Ms. Fleck's carelessness shows indifference to her obligations to her former clients and to the State Bar, have frustrated the investigation of this matter, and thus, constitutes a willful violation of Section 6068.

For the above reasons, the State Bar will be able to prevail on this charge against Ms. Fleck.

February 2016

California Bar Examination

Performance Test B
INSTRUCTIONS AND FILE

JAY MINOR v. LUCINDA MINOR

JAY MINOR v. LUCINDA MINOR

INSTRUCTIONS

1. This performance test is designed to evaluate your ability to handle a select number of legal authorities in the context of a factual problem involving a client.

2. The problem is set in the fictional State of Columbia, one of the United States.

3. You will have two sets of materials with which to work: a File and a Library.

4. The File contains factual materials about your case. The first document is a memorandum containing the instructions for the tasks you are to complete.

5. The Library contains the legal authorities needed to complete the tasks. The case reports may be real, modified, or written solely for the purpose of this performance test. If the cases appear familiar to you, do not assume that they are precisely the same as you have read before. Read each thoroughly, as if it were new to you. You should assume that cases were decided in the jurisdictions and on the dates shown. In citing cases from the Library, you may use abbreviations and omit page citations.

6. You should concentrate on the materials provided, but you should also bring to bear on the problem your general knowledge of the law. What you have learned in law school and elsewhere provides the general background for analyzing the problem; the File and Library provide the specific materials with which you must work.

7. Although there are no parameters on how to apportion your time, you should allow yourself sufficient time to thoroughly review the materials and organize your planned response.

8. Your response will be graded on its compliance with instructions and on its content, thoroughness, and organization.

O'HALLARAN, MEYER & JENSON

224 Court Street
Hamilton, Columbia

MEMORANDUM

TO: Applicant

FROM: Sharon Jenson

DATE: February 25, 2016

RE: Jay Minor v. Lucinda Minor

We represent Lucinda Minor ("Luci") opposing a post-dissolution motion filed against her by her ex-husband, Jay Minor. We had represented her during the dissolution three years ago, which the parties settled through mediation. They had one son, who was an adult at the time. The agreement divided the marital estate equally, and both parties waived their claims for spousal support.

Jay has filed a Motion to Modify the Settlement Agreement, alleging that the agreement rested on a mutual mistake, together with a motion to exclude the testimony of the parties and the mediator about what the parties said during the mediation.

Please draft a persuasive Memorandum of Points and Authorities rebutting Jay Minor's contentions, both as to mutual mistake and as to mediation confidentiality.

O'HALLARAN, MEYER & JENSON

224 Court Street

Hamilton, Columbia

MEMORANDUM

TO: All Attorneys

FROM: Executive Committee

RE: Persuasive Briefs and Memoranda

In drafting persuasive briefs, the firm conforms to the following guidelines:

Except when there is already an agreed or stipulated identification of the facts, the briefs should begin with a short and concise Statement of Facts, using only those facts supported by the record. The Statement of Facts is not an indiscriminate recitation of all the facts in the case. Include only those facts you need for your persuasive arguments. Although the facts must be stated accurately, careful selection of the ones pertinent to the legal arguments and that support our client is not improper.

The firm follows the practice of writing carefully crafted subject headings which illustrate the arguments they cover. The Argument section of the brief should contain separate segments, each labeled with headings that summarize the argument in the ensuing segment. Do not write a brief that contains only a single broad heading. Each heading should succinctly state the reasons why the tribunal should adopt the position you are advocating and not merely a bare legal or factual proposition.

The body of each argument should match the relevant facts to the legal authorities and argue persuasively how the facts as applied to those authorities support our client's position. Authority that favors our client should be emphasized, but contrary authority should be addressed in the argument and distinguished or explained, not ignored. Do not reserve argument for reply or supplemental briefs.

You need not prepare a table of contents, a table of cases, a summary of the argument, or an index. These will be prepared after the draft is approved.

NOTES ON INTERVIEW WITH LUCINDA (LUCI) MINOR

February 11, 2016

I met with Luci Minor today about her ex-husband's recent efforts to claw back some money out of their dissolution settlement. Her ex-husband, Jay Minor, has hired Joe Gaines to file a Motion to Modify the Settlement, as well as a motion to exclude certain testimony.

In the original settlement, Luci got the main house here in Hamilton, her own pension, and an additional $200,000 taken out of their main investment account. Jay got the vacation home at the lake, his own pension, and the balance of the investment account, worth an additional $300,000 at the time. She says that the papers seem to represent that much accurately.

According to her, her long-standing doubts about the investment account turned out to be true. Beginning about 15 years ago, Jay started investing with Saint Gaudens Investments ("SG"), based on a friend's recommendations that SG was producing returns that were well above market for a sustained period. Jay hoped that SG could help him fund their son, Jay Jr.'s, college education. (Jay Jr. had graduated at the time of the dissolution and was paying his way through grad school at the time.) SG did help out with that, and brought extraordinary returns, substantially increasing Jay's initial investment by the time of the dissolution.

However, Luci never believed that SG was for real. It was "too much of too good to be true," in her words. She never said as much to Jay, but by the time of the dissolution, she wanted out. That was why, in mediation, she insisted that Jay take over the SG account, and that she cash out as much as was needed to equalize their shares. Also in mediation, she told Jay that he should get out too.

What she remembers specifically is that in the mediation, she told Jay that SG had slowed down in recent years. She also told Jay that she had heard several fairly reliable rumors that major investors in SG were beginning to cash out in full. She said that she didn't want to take any risks with SG, and wanted cash. Jay said that he had heard those same rumors, but that he had investigated them, and had talked with Theodore Saint Gaudens, head of SG. He said that he was more than happy to take his chances, and that she would come to regret not keeping her money "where it would do the most work."

Luci is confident that the mediator will recall the conversation going exactly as she recalls it. How to handle the SG account was the major focus of their settlement discussions.

After the settlement, Jay withdrew the $200,000 from SG and paid it to Luci promptly.

A little over a year ago, she said that SG crashed. She heard about it first from one of the friends who had advised her at the time of the dissolution, and then she heard it on the news. Then she heard from Jay. He said that he now realizes that the account had been bad all along, and that, as far as he was concerned, the account had a zero value, not only now, but back at the time of the dissolution. He then asked her for $150,000. He said that they had always agreed that they should split things evenly. Without the SG money in the picture, she ended up with $300,000 more than he had at the time of the dissolution, and that a $150,000 payment would make them square.

Luci rejected him, quickly and angrily. She reminded him of what he said during the mediation, and said that she bet that the mediator would back her up. He threatened her with a lawsuit, and she said, "Fine."

SETTLEMENT AGREEMENT

Jay Simon Minor (the "Husband") and Lucinda Elaine Minor (the "Wife") enter into this Settlement Agreement as a full and final resolution of all claims between them arising out of their dissolution.

. . . . .

4. The Wife will receive as her share of the marital estate the following assets:

-- the parties' principal residence in Hamilton, Columbia, valued for purposes of this agreement at $200,000.

-- all of the value in her pension accounts as listed in the appendix to this agreement, valued for purposes of this agreement at $200,000.

5. The Husband will receive as his share of the marital estate the following assets:

-- the parties' vacation residence in Lakes County, Columbia, valued for purposes of this agreement at $100,000.

-- all of the value in his pension accounts as listed in the appendix to this agreement, valued for purposes of this agreement at $200,000.

-- the entire value of the parties' investment account with Saint Gaudens Investments, valued for purposes of this agreement at $500,000. The wife will execute whatever documentation is required to transfer sole ownership of this investment account to the Husband.

6. The parties intend that they each receive one-half of the entire marital estate. In furtherance of this goal, the Husband agrees that, within two months of the final decree in this dissolution, he will withdraw $200,000 from the investment account with Saint Gaudens Investments, and transfer that amount in cash to the Wife.

Joseph Gaines

GAINES, HOYT & STEPHENS, LLC

24 City Square

Hamilton, Columbia

Attorneys for Petitioner, Jay Simon Minor

IN THE SUPERIOR COURT OF HAMILTON COUNTY

STATE OF COLUMBIA

JAY SIMON MINOR, Petitioner, v. LUCINDA ELAINE MINOR, Respondent.	Docket No. 43-4443 MEMORANDUM OF POINTS AND AUTHORITIES IN SUPPORT OF MOTION TO MODIFY SETTLEMENT AGREEMENT AND TO EXCLUDE EVIDENCE

I. FACTS

Petitioner and Respondent received a dissolution from each other by final decree of this court, dated April 20, 2013. In a Settlement Agreement, the parties divided total assets with an approximate value of $1,200,000. The parties agreed that each party should get an equal share of those assets, or $600,000. As part of the marital estate, the parties discussed ownership of what they believed to be an account at the investment firm of Saint Gaudens Investments ("SG"). At the time of their agreement, they believed that account to hold roughly $500,000 in investment securities. Petitioner received the entire value of that account as part of his share. To equalize the values of each party's share, the parties agreed that Petitioner would withdraw $200,000 from the SG account and transfer that amount in cash to Respondent. Petitioner accomplished this withdrawal and transfer within two months after the final decree of this court.

Thirteen months ago, Petitioner received notice from the Securities and Exchange Commission that the head of SG, Theodore Saint Gaudens, had been arrested for securities fraud. Petitioner learned that, for over 17 years, Saint Gaudens had been using SG to run a "Ponzi scheme." Under such a scheme, investments by current investors are used to pay returns to earlier investors, at rates of return well in excess of market averages. Twelve months ago, Petitioner received a preliminary accounting of the assets of SG, which indicated that the firm did not have and had never had any significant assets at any one time. Subsequent accountings of SG indicate that the total amounts entrusted to the firm came to over $150,000,000, and that none of the present investors in SG would receive any portion of their investments.

On information and belief, Petitioner understands that Respondent intends to call the mediator as a witness in connection with Petitioner's Motion to Modify.

II. ARGUMENT

Petitioner requests that the court find that the parties entered into their Settlement Agreement in this case based on a mutual mistake. Petitioner and Respondent entered into their settlement agreement based on the belief that they would be able to recover funds that they had invested in SG, and indeed that those funds were available in full as of the date of the settlement. That belief was mistaken: An account as such did not exist at SG, and all of the funds invested by Petitioner and Respondent had been used to pay off earlier investors. Both Petitioner and Respondent suffered from the identical mistaken belief about the nature and reliability of the SG account at the time of the settlement agreement. The belief resulted in an allocation of $500,000 in value to Petitioner, and a transfer of $200,000 to Respondent, out of an estate that totaled (without the SG "holdings") no more than $700,000.

Petitioner thus requests that the court reform the Settlement Agreement to require the equalization of the parties' share at the time of the settlement agreement, without considering the value assigned to the SG investment account.

A. The Parties' Mistake About the Existence of the Funds in the SG Account Existed at the Time of the Settlement Agreement.

The allegations in this motion provide a sufficiently specific basis on which the court can make a finding of mutual mistake. *Snyder v. Abrams* (Col. S. Ct. 2008). The mistake about the existence of the SG investment account existed at the time of the Settlement Agreement. At the time, both Petitioner and Respondent believed that the SG investment firm operated as a legitimate investment company, and that either or both of them would have the right to withdraw their funds in full from the account at any time, then or in the future. In fact, SG was nothing more than a Ponzi scheme, with all of the funds paid in by the parties already paid out to other earlier investors to generate the impression of favorable returns. As a result, Petitioner's request comports with Columbia law, which requires that allegations of mutual mistake focus solely on mistakes existing "at the time the parties entered into the stipulation." *Nathanson v. Nathanson* (Col. Ct. App. 2010).

B. The Existence and Availability of the Funds in the SG Investment Account Represent a Central Element of the Parties' Settlement Discussions.

Moreover, the facts at issue are material, if not central, to the parties' negotiation. *Snyder v. Abrams* (Col. S. Ct. 2008). Even including, for purposes of argument, the value of the SG "holdings", the total value of the marital estate came to $1,200,000, of which those "holdings" constituted $500,000. Removal of that value from the negotiations would have had a substantial impact on the discussions. Moreover, it seems beyond question that, had the parties both known of the fact that SG operated a Ponzi scheme, they would have negotiated a different settlement.

C. The Mistake in This Case Relates to Facts Existing at the Time of the Settlement, Not to Future Valuation of Assets or Uncertain Future Events.

This case does not present a mere dispute over future fluctuations in the valuation of assets; *see Edwards v. Edwards* (Col. Ct. App. 1985). Nor is it the same as those cases in which the parties were mistaken over an event that could not occur until some time in the future. *Laramee v. Laramee* (Col. Ct. App. 1972) (no mutual mistake where parties agreed to payments based on a future retirement date that later changed). Rather, this case presents a unique case, where the parties believed an asset existed that in fact did not exist.

D. Testimony About Statements Made During Mediation Between the Parties Only Prove the Amount of Claim and Should Not Be Admitted.

The parties' Settlement Agreement is unambiguous in establishing the parties' intentions to divide their existing marital estate equally between them. In the absence of ambiguity, the mediator's testimony thus constitutes inadmissible extrinsic evidence. *Blalock v. Gross* (Col. S. Ct. 2008). The mediator's testimony will only serve to highlight the parties' discussions as to the size of the share to be allocated to each party pursuant to the agreement. It constitutes information sought to prove "the amount of the claim" and is thus inadmissible under Mediation Rule 2.11. *Blalock v. Gross* (Col. S. Ct. 2008).

For these reasons, and for the reasons stated in the foregoing statement of facts, Petitioner seeks reformation of the contract in accordance with his pleading, on the ground of mutual mistake, and requests that this court bar the admission of any testimony from the parties or the mediator about statements made by the parties during the mediation leading up to the parties' final settlement agreement.

DATE: February 8, 2016   GAINES, HOYT & STEPHENS, LLC

                                          By: *Joseph Gaines*

                                          Joseph Gaines

                                          Attorneys for Petitioner,

                                          Jay Simon Minor

February 2016

California
Bar
Examination

Performance Test B

LIBRARY

JAY MINOR v. LUCINDA MINOR

LIBRARY

COLUMBIA MEDIATION RULES

Rule 2.11. **Compromise and Offers to Compromise**

Evidence of conduct or statements by any party or mediator at a mediation session is not admissible to prove liability for, invalidity of, or amount of the claim or any other claim. Such evidence may be admitted to prove or disprove fraud, duress, or other cause to invalidate the mediation result in the proceeding with respect to which the mediation was held or in any other proceeding between the parties to the mediation that involves the subject matter of the mediation.

Snyder v. Abrams

Columbia Supreme Court (2008)

Sidney Snyder and Janeen Abrams married on May 26, 1991, and received a dissolution from a judgment dated March 28, 2005. The judgment of dissolution incorporated the parties' stipulation of settlement (hereinafter the "Agreement"), executed on February 2, 2005. The Agreement provides, in relevant part, that Snyder's stock awards from his employer, Alpine Investments Inc. ("Alpine"), would be "divided 50–50 in kind." The Agreement specified that 3,800 shares of the stock awards were available for division and allocated 1,900 shares to Abrams.

Abrams then sold her 1,900 shares. Later, Snyder learned that only 150 shares remained. According to an affidavit attached to Snyder's motion to modify, the number of shares on which the parties premised the Agreement (3,800) constituted the gross number of delivered and outstanding shares available prior to the payment of taxes, fees, and other withholdings. Alpine used a significant number of the total number of gross shares to pay taxes and fees, and make other withholdings. The net number of shares available for division by the parties thus totaled only 2,050.

Abrams rejected Snyder's demand that she remit to him the shares or the value thereof in excess of her 50% share. Snyder then commenced the instant action, eventually moving for summary judgment. Snyder argued that a mutual mistake led the parties to use the gross number of shares, 3,800, instead of the accurate number of 2,050. The plaintiff accordingly sought reformation of the agreement to reflect the net number of shares actually available for division.

Abrams opposed the motion, arguing that the only mistake had been made by Snyder.

Snyder's motion for summary judgment was granted by the trial court.

Under Columbia law, settlement agreements in dissolution cases constitute independent contracts, subject to the principles of contract law. The parties may not seek relief from their own agreement, unless they can establish cause sufficient to invalidate a contract, such as fraud, collusion, mistake or accident. The party seeking to demonstrate any of these grounds bears a heightened burden of proof, and must establish them by clear and convincing evidence.

To reform a settlement agreement on the ground of mutual mistake, a party must demonstrate that the mistake existed at the time the parties entered into the stipulation. *Baker v. Baker* (Col. Ct. App. 1995) (affirming finding of mistake where parties later discovered that a restrictive covenant barred subdivision of real estate to be subdivided pursuant to the agreement); *Franciosa v. Marinelli* (Col. Ct. App. 1998) (affirming finding of mistake where parties later discovered that a pension earned as a public employee could not be transferred).

Moreover, the mistaken fact must form so substantial a premise for the agreement that the stipulation does not represent a true meeting of the parties' minds. The alleged mistake must involve a fundamental assumption of the contract, in the sense that the mistake vitally affects the facts that form the basis of the parties' contract. Here, Snyder has established a prima facie case of mutual mistake. Both the final agreement and all five earlier drafts refer to the gross number of shares as available for division. Snyder repeatedly generated summaries of those shares in his capacity as an Alpine employee, and routinely shared those summaries with Abrams. Abrams concedes that both parties and their attorneys relied on those summaries throughout the negotiations.

However, neither the parties nor their counsel apparently realized that the number of 3,800 shares that they were using represented the gross shares, not the net shares Alpine would deliver after it paid taxes and fees, and made other withholdings. Due diligence might have advised that their attorneys pin down the net number of shares with greater precision. We have held that where information to correct a mistake is readily available, one party may not hold out the mistake as a reason for invalidating the agreement. And of course, unilateral mistake does not constitute a ground for reforming an agreement.

In this case, the parties used the figure of 3,800 shares throughout their negotiations, without question from either side. This constituted a mutual mistake that undermined their intent to divide the net shares available for division.

The trial court correctly focused the inquiry on the parties' intention as indicated in their language that the shares be "divided 50–50 in kind." A practical interpretation of this language supports the conclusion that the parties intended "in kind" to mean actual shares or their equivalent monetary value.

The trial court correctly reformed the agreement to refer to the net shares available for division, and to provide that each party should receive one-half of those net shares or their equivalent monetary value.

Affirmed.

Nathanson v. Nathanson

Columbia Court of Appeal (2010)

This appeal requires us to determine whether the trial court erred in reforming a provision in the parties' dissolution settlement agreement on the ground of mutual mistake. The parties had agreed that Respondent would promptly receive the proceeds from the sale of stock held in a privately-owned bank. Two years later, the sale had not occurred, the bank had failed, and the stock had no market or discernible value.

George and Verna Nathanson (respectively "Husband" and "Wife") married in 1978, and received a dissolution in 2007. They had two children, both adults at the time of the dissolution. During the marriage, they enjoyed a prosperous lifestyle. Their 2005 income tax return listed more than $3,000,000 in earned and unearned income for the year. Filings in their dissolution in 2007 total gross assets of nearly $19,000,000, and joint monthly expenses of $44,000. The dissolution required disposition of numerous assets acquired during the marriage, including the marital home, a beach house, several vehicles, and many stocks, mutual funds, and investment accounts.

With the aid of their attorneys, the parties entered into a Property Settlement Agreement, which was then incorporated into a final judgment of dissolution entered on May 23, 2007. This Agreement explicitly provided that equitable distribution of the parties' assets substituted for any obligation of the husband to pay spousal support. Husband was expressly relieved from any current or future application for spousal support based on an understanding that the assets distributed to Wife would provide the income she needed to maintain her economic status and lifestyle.

Paragraph twenty-seven of the agreement listed eighteen accounts and securities with a total value of more than $4,100,000 as assets to be retained by or conveyed to Wife exclusively. Among the eighteen assets was a listing for 62,000 shares of stock with a stated value of $1,085,000 in privately-owned Aeolian Bank. Two handwritten notations accompanied the designation of this asset: the words "sale directed on 5–18–07" written alongside the listing, and a footnote that stated "Salesman has been directed that the proceeds be promptly wired to the Wife." No other asset included any similar notation or footnote.

Husband said a call had been placed to William Decker (the president of Aeolian Bank) at the time of the settlement conference directing him to sell the stock, and that Wife and the attorneys were present during the call. Decker stated over a speaker phone that the Bank had purchased a large number of its own shares earlier that month and agreed that the parties' holdings would then be listed at $1.085 million.

Two years after the dissolution, Wife filed a motion to enforce the parties' Agreement as to the Aeolian Bank stock, and directing defendant to sell that stock immediately. Husband opposed the motion, declaring that he had fulfilled his obligation under the settlement agreement, that the Aeolian Bank had gone out of business, and that the stock had no value.

Based on this testimony, the trial court found that the parties operated on the basis of a mutual mistake about the marketability and ultimately the value of the Aeolian Bank stock at the time of entering into the settlement agreement. It found that the parties had the specific intent that Wife would get the proceeds of the Aeolian Bank stock sale that had been directed on 5/18/07 "promptly wired" to her. It noted that both parties and the nonparty witness believed as of May 18, 2007, that the stock had a particular value and was immediately marketable. Contrary to this belief, the court found that both parties were mistaken in thinking that the total value of their marital estate was $1.085 million more than it actually was.

Finally, the trial court reformed the relevant provisions of the settlement agreement. The trial court found that each party should bear the consequences of the mistake equally.

No genuine dispute exists regarding the parties' meaning and their intent with respect to distribution of the Aeolian Bank stock. The unique notations appended to the listing of the Aeolian Bank stock in the settlement agreement showed the parties intended to sell that stock immediately and transfer the proceeds promptly to Wife, providing her with about $1,085,000 in cash. Although Husband correctly argues that he did not guarantee the stock could be sold for that amount and at that time, he does not credibly dispute the parties' intention.

Husband argues that a finding of mutual mistake requires that both parties agree when they attempt to reduce their understanding to writing, but that the writing does not express the understanding correctly. He contends that he was not mistaken, because he did not believe that that the stock would be immediately sold for the $1,085,000 asking price. But this argument misstates the basis of the trial court's ruling. The court found that the parties intended to provide $1,085,000 in cash proceeds to Wife, but mistakenly thought that their intent could be accomplished by the prompt sale of the Aeolian Bank stock. They did not intend to distribute the Aeolian Bank stock to Wife as an investment asset.

Finally, Husband argues that Columbia prevents a finding of mutual mistake, where the mistake relates to a <u>future</u> fact. At the time of the dissolution, Husband contends, neither party anticipated that Aeolian Bank would fail, nor could they have done so. According to Husband, to reform an agreed-upon division of assets when one of the assets later becomes valueless directly contravenes the parties' own allocation of risks and benefits in their settlement agreement. In this case, Husband contends that Wife accepted and should bear the entire risk of Aeolian's failure.

Husband correctly notes that our courts do not generally reform dissolution agreements for mistakes relating to future events. For example, in *Laramee v. Laramee* (Col. Ct. App. 1972), the spouses agreed that the "Husband will pay one-half of his Civil Service Retirement payments to the Wife" when he retired. The wife assumed that the husband would retire at age 65, but he did not. The Court of Appeal refused to reform, noting that "mistaken expectations about the future are not grounds to set aside or reform a contract -- the mistake must relate to a past or present material fact."

Similarly, in *Edwards v. Edwards* (Col. Ct. App. 1985), a trial court refused to reform a division of property when, within months of the final decree, a rezoning decision substantially raised the value of a significant asset. The Court of Appeal affirmed, stating that "to vacate a stipulation of settlement on the ground of mutual mistake, [a party must] demonstrate that the mistake existed at the time of the stipulation." In its view, the mere possibility of a future rise (or fall) in the value of an asset did justify a finding of mutual mistake.

These cases all involve situations where, through settlement agreements, the parties clearly and specifically allocated and accepted the risks associated with future events. The critical inquiry in all of these cases focused on the parties' intentions at the time of contracting. Where the parties' intentions are clear, but where they have mistakenly selected means that make it impossible to carry out those intentions, the court may reform the contract to carry out the parties' goals.

In the case at hand, the trial court found that the parties intended that Wife would receive a cash payout of $1,085,000 from the sale of the Aeolian Bank stock. The court also found that the parties did not intend that Wife would receive the stock itself as an investment. These findings necessarily imply that the parties did not allocate to the Wife the risk of future fluctuations in the value of the stock, nor the complete failure of the Bank. Instead, Husband assumed these risks, by agreeing to assure the sale of the stock so as to produce the agreed-upon cash payout.

We find no basis to overturn the trial court's ruling.

Affirmed.

Blalock v. Gross

Columbia Supreme Court (2008)

On December 31, 1996, Wife and Husband were married, and on October 3, 2001, Wife filed a petition for dissolution. On March 21, 2002, Wife and Husband took part in a mediation of the final settlement of their dissolution action, resulting in the Agreement. The trial court approved the Agreement and entered it as part of the final decree on March 22, 2002.

The Agreement provided in part that Husband would give Wife an interest in a Promissory Note, secured by a mortgage on newly constructed residential real estate. Husband retained ownership of the real estate, and agreed to pay Wife's interest in the Promissory Note out of the proceeds of sale, when the real estate sold.

The Promissory Note reads as follows: "Borrower [Husband] is to pay the sum of Twenty-three Thousand Dollars ($23,000) and the total of all documented construction costs, not to exceed Eighty Thousand Dollars ($80,000)." The note further requires that the proceeds of sale were to go into escrow pending resolution of all claims to the proceeds.

On February 6, 2003, Husband sold the property for a selling price of $115,000. On the same date, Husband paid Wife $23,000. Husband placed $92,000, the balance of the proceeds, into escrow.

Wife then filed a motion to enforce judgment, arguing that she should receive an additional $80,000 from the amounts in escrow. In reply, Husband argued that the Agreement and the Promissory Note unambiguously awarded only $23,000 to Wife, allocating the balance of any proceeds to him.

At hearing, both the parties and the mediator who drafted the Agreement testified. The trial court concluded that Wife had a contractual right only to $23,000. This appeal followed.

Wife contends that the trial court erred when it admitted the testimony of the mediator to resolve the alleged ambiguity in the agreement. We agree. No ambiguity exists in the Agreement which might justify the taking of extrinsic evidence concerning its terms. Moreover, to the extent that any ambiguity exists, Columbia's Mediation Rules bar the introduction of the mediator's testimony on this issue.

General principles of contract law govern settlement agreements in the same way as any other agreement. A court should enforce a settlement agreement if the contract contains no ambiguities and if the court can discern the parties' intent from the written terms. Absent an ambiguity, the terms themselves control. We do not construe the contract or look to extrinsic evidence, but will merely apply the contractual provisions.

Here, the note requires Husband to pay Wife "the sum of Twenty-three Thousand Dollars ($23,000) and the total of all documented construction costs, not to exceed Eighty Thousand Dollars ($80,000)."

At trial, the court permitted testimony from the mediator about the parties' conversations concerning this particular Promissory Note. Testifying from his notes of the mediation sessions, the mediator stated that the parties continually referred to the Note as "the $23K Note", and discussed what would happen when Husband paid Wife the $23,000 stated on the face of the Note. In addition, the mediator testified that it was his understanding, based on the parties' discussions, that Wife "was to receive $23,000" from the Note.

This testimony appears to contradict the unambiguous language of the Agreement and the Promissory Note. The Note specifically entitles Wife to receive both $23,000 and up to $80,000 in construction costs. Nothing in the Agreement or in the Note contradicts this outcome. The parties unambiguously expressed their intention that Wife should receive up to $103,000 upon the sale of the property. The trial court erred in finding otherwise.

Given the lack of ambiguity in the Agreement, we could resolve this case with a finding that the admission of the mediator's testimony as extrinsic evidence was itself in error. However, important policy considerations compel us to state an additional ground for our decision.

Mediation Rule 2.11 of the Columbia Mediation Rules states that statements by any party at a mediation "is not admissible to prove liability for, invalidity of, or amount of the claim or any other claim", but "may be admitted to prove fraud, duress, or other cause to invalidate the mediation result."

Here, Husband called the mediator as a witness in an attempt to establish the amount of the claim, in contravention of the foregoing mediation rule. The trial court's decision to permit this testimony thus directly contravenes Rule 2.11.

Husband contends that the disparity in the parties' contentions concerning the amount owed to Wife constitutes a "cause to invalidate the mediation result" under Rule 2.11. Husband's argument must fail. The listed grounds for "invalidation" include fraud, duress, or "other cause" for invalidation. The clear tenor of this list focuses on grounds for invalidation, and includes such other grounds as mutual mistake or unconscionability. In all these cases, parties may avail themselves of the mediator's testimony for purposes of resolving a present issue about the validity of the agreement itself, and of seeking the court's aid in reforming or rescinding the contract.

In this case, Husband has consistently pled and argued the ambiguity of the underlying contract, and used that ambiguity as grounds for introducing extrinsic evidence in support of his interpretation. Ambiguity may represent an interpretive challenge for any court in reading a contract. But under the law, a finding of ambiguity merely permits the court to consider other information in interpreting the contract. It does not give rise to the same "invalidation" that the grounds stated and implied that Rule 2.11 might support.

Mediation offers a vital tool to parties and to the courts in resolving disputes. We have long expressed the opinion that evidentiary protection for statements made during mediation facilitate candor in important negotiations that rely on the sharing of sensitive information. Rule 2.11 encourages litigants to speak freely in mediation without the concern that statements made while pursuing settlement through mediation would be used at a trial on the merits if the mediation failed. The same considerations apply when one party seeks to undo the work that both parties have done in mediation, especially when that work produces an unambiguous result.

The trial court erred in permitting the mediator to testify to the parties' discussions in mediation, and in relying on that testimony in reaching its result.

Reversed.

PT-B: SELECTED ANSWER 1

Memorandum of Points and Authorities in Support of Respondent Lucinda Elaine Minor's Opposition to
Petitioner Jay Simon Minor's Motion to Modify Settlement Agreement and to Exclude Evidence

Respondent, Lucinda Elaine Minor ("Luci"), by her undersigned counsel, submits this Memorandum of Points and Authorities in Support of her Opposition to Petitioner Jay Simon Minor's ("Jay") Motion to Modify Settlement Agreement and to Exclude Evidence (the "Motion") and, in support thereof, states as follows:

I. STATEMENT OF FACTS

This case presents a straightforward circumstance in which one party to a Settlement Agreement (the "Agreement"), Jay, is no longer satisfied with the terms that he negotiated before entering into the Agreement in connection with the dissolution of his marriage to Luci. Under the Agreement, Luci received the parties' principal residence in Hamilton, Columbia (valued at $200K) and her pension accounts (also valued at $200k). Jay received the parties' Lake House (valued at $100K) and his pension account (valued at $200K). The sole remaining "asset," and that at issue here, was the parties' Saint Gaudens Investment ("SG") account, purportedly valued at $500K. To achieve an equal division of marital assets, Jay agreed to withdraw $200K from this account and pay it to Luci within 2 months of the agreement. This resulted in a $600K split for both Luci and Jay.

However, Luci specifically communicated during mediation that she had no desire to retain any portion of the SG account because she had serious doubts about the viability of the account and the monetary assets purportedly housed therein. Luci never believed that SG was legitimate because, according to her, "it was too much of too good to be true." Consequently, while the parties were dividing marital assets at mediation, Luci insisted that Jay take over the SG account and commented during mediation that she had heard several fairly reliable rumors that major investors were cashing out and that holding assets there any longer was very risky. Although Jay acknowledged hearing these same rumors, he claimed to have investigated them and spoken to the head of SG who allayed any concerns. Thus, Jay told Luci that he was "more than happy to take his chances, and that she would come to regret not keeping her money 'where it would do the most work.'" Jay's disregard for obvious risks of insolvency was apparent to both Luci and the mediator, who is expected to testify to confirm Luci's account of her mediation communications to Jay about the risks and likely insolvency of the SG account.

After the Agreement was executed, Jay promptly withdrew $200K and paid it to Luci, as required under the Agreement. However, as Luci predicted, SG thereafter crashed and became insolvent. Jay now seeks to recover from Luci $150K, representing half of the $300K that he was "more than happy to take his chances" with, claiming that he is entitled to recover half of his loss from Luci because the parties intended to divide their assets equally and that neither the parties nor mediator should be permitted to testify about Luci's concern and statements during mediation about the SG account. As detailed more fully below, Jay's Motion should be denied.

II. ARGUMENT

A. The Parties' Agreement Should Not be Invalidated Because Jay Cannot Meet His Burden to Prove by Clear and Convincing Evidence that the Parties' Agreement Was Based Upon a Mutual Mistake of Material Fact as all Parties Were Aware of the Risks of SG's Insolvency and Jay Willingly and Proudly Assumed that Risk in Entering into the Agreement.

Under Columbia law, settlement agreements in dissolution cases are deemed independent contracts and, as such, are subject to the principles of contract law. *Snyder 2008.* Parties to these settlement agreements may not seek relief from their agreements unless they can establish sufficient cause, such as fraud, collusion, mistake or accident. The party seeking to invalidate the settlement agreement "bears a heightened burden of proof, and must establish [these causes] by clear and convincing evidence." *Id.*

Here, Jay seeks to invalidate the agreement on the ground that the agreement was based upon a mutual mistake of material fact. In order to prevail on this theory, Jay must demonstrate (1) that the mistake existed at the time the parties entered into the Agreement (*Snyder*, citing *Baker 1995* (finding mistake where parties were unaware of restrictive covenant barring subdivision of real estate) and *Franciosa 1998* (finding mistake where parties later discovered that pension could not be transferred)); (2) that the mistaken fact involves a fundamental assumption of the contract and forms a substantial premise for the parties' agreement (*Snyder*); and (3) that the mistake did not relate to a future event (*Nathanson*, citing *Laramee* and *Edwards*). Failure to satisfy any one of these elements renders Jay's Motion inadequate. As detailed more fully below, Jay cannot demonstrate any of these elements, let alone all of these elements, by clear and convincing evidence and, accordingly, Jay's Motion should be denied.

1. There Existed No Mutual Mistake About the Existence of the Funds in the SG Account at the Time of the Agreement Because Luci Doubted that the SG Account Contained Any Funds.

To support this element of his claim, Jay erroneously contends that at the time of the Agreement, both he and Luci "believed that the SG investment firm operated as a legitimate investment company" and that they could withdraw funds from their SG account at any time, "then or in the future." *Jay's Mot.* at 13. This is factually incorrect.

Rather, Luci held long-standing doubts about the SG account dating back to the time that Jay initially invested with SG and never believed that SG was legitimate or for real. Although she did not previously communicate this belief to Jay, she wanted out by the time of mediation and insisted that Jay take over the SG account and suggested that he get out. As stated above, she advised Jay of the rumors about SG's potential insolvency, and that she did not want to take any risks with SG. Thus, it is clear that, contrary to Jay's contention, Luci did not believe that SG was reputable or that the parties could withdraw any funds from SG.

Jay cites *Nathanson* to support this element, but that case is easily distinguishable. In *Nathanson*, the parties listed a specific account in their agreement believing that one of the accounts contained shares of stock valued over $1 million. The husband was directed to liquidate that stock and pay the money to the ex-wife. It was not intended as an investment account. When the husband failed to do so, and the stock thereafter lost all value, the Court reformed the parties' agreement because the parties were mutually mistaken in believing that their intent to provide $1 million plus to the ex-wife could be accomplished by the sale of the stock. Consequently, the ex-wife's mutual mistake argument was upheld, and the trial court's reformation was upheld.

Conversely, in this case, the only mistake that occurred was Jay's belief that retaining $300K in the SG account was a prudent investment. Luci was well aware that it was not, and Luci advised Jay accordingly. As a result, Luci negotiated an express term in the settlement agreement requiring Jay to promptly liquidate $200K of the SG account and pay her, which he did. *Nathanson* is therefore inapposite, and not persuasive. As Jay cannot meet his burden to prove this element by clear and convincing evidence, his Motion should be denied.

2. The Solvency of the SG Account Was Not a Fundamental Assumption of the Parties' Agreement.

Jay again incorrectly assumes, without any clear and convincing evidence, that the value of the SG account was a "central element" of the parties' Agreement and settlement discussions. In support of this argument, Jay merely claims that the alleged $500K value of the SG account was a substantial portion of the $1.2 million marital assets at issue and that removing the SG account from the negotiation would have substantially impacted the discussions. He claims, again without any supporting evidence, that the parties would have negotiated a different settlement if "the parties both [had] known of the fact that SG operated a Ponzi scheme."

Jay cites *Snyder* in passing in support of this element, but the facts of *Snyder* are easily distinguishable. In that case, the parties exchanged 5 drafts and a final agreement referencing the 3,800 shares of stock they believed were available for distribution. Moreover, Mr. Snyder repeatedly generated summaries of the shares of available stock, and both parties and their counsel reviewed and relied on those summaries throughout the negotiation. Despite these facts, neither party nor their counsel ever realized that there were in fact only 2,050 shares available for distribution, although due diligence would have likely revealed these facts. Accordingly, the Court concluded that both parties relied on the 3,800 shares figure throughout negotiations without question by either side and, therefore, this constituted a mutual mistake that undermined their intent to divide the assets evenly.

Conversely, there were no similar back and forth exchanges between Jay and Luci here. Rather, there was one set of negotiations on the day of the mediation during which time Luci made perfectly clear that she did not believe the SG account was for real, that she questioned SG's solvency, that there were reliable rumors causing legitimate concern, and that Jay should get out of SG as well. Jay rejected all of these remarks and instead chose to keep his money in at his own risk. Even *Snyder* recognized that "where information to correct a mistake is readily available, one party may not hold out the mistake as a reason for invalidating the agreement." Here, unlike Snyder, there was ample information available to Jay to correct his unilateral mistaken belief of the solvency of SG, and he cannot claim otherwise.

Moreover, to the extent that Jay claims that only he was mistaken on this "central element" during the parties' negotiation, *Snyder* expressly recognized that a "unilateral mistake does not constitute a ground for reforming an agreement." Although Jay's mistake (if he was even mistaken) is unilateral given that Luci was clearly not mistaken on this issue, such a mistake does not allow for reformation under these circumstances.

Ultimately, Jay has offered little, if any, evidence to support his contention that the existence and availability of funds in the SG account was a fundamental assumption or substantial premise upon which the parties' agreement was based. Accordingly, he certainly has failed to meet his burden to prove this element by "clear and convincing evidence," as he must in order to prevail. Finally, even if Jay succeeds on this element, his Motion should be denied because he cannot establish the first or third required elements, as detailed above and below.

3. Jay's Unilateral Mistake Relates to a Future Fact or Event (SG's Insolvency), Not a Past or Existing Fact, and Therefore Does Not Support His Request for Reformation.

It is well-settled Columbia law that "courts do not generally reform dissolution agreements for mistakes relating to future events." Courts in this jurisdiction have repeatedly refused reformation where the request was based on alleged mistakes about future facts or events. For example, in *Laramee*, the Court refused reformation where the spouses agreed that the husband would pay one-half of his retirement benefits to the wife when he retired, but he thereafter did not retire by the age of 65 as the wife assumed he would. The Court noted that "mistaken expectations about the future are not grounds to set aside or reform a contract -- the mistake must relate to a past or present material fact." *Nathanson* (citing *Laramee*).

Similarly, in *Edwards*, the Court affirmed a trial court order denying reformation where a rezoning decision rendered months after the final decree substantially raised the value of a significant asset. There, the Court stated that "'to vacate a stipulation of settlement on the ground of mutual mistake, [a party must] demonstrate that the mistake existed at the time of the stipulation.'" *Id.* (citing *Edwards*). In the *Edwards* Court's view, "the mere possibility of a future rise (or fall) in the value of an asset did not justify a finding of mutual mistake." *Id.*

As *Nathanson* points out, these cases where reformation has been denied for mistakes of future fact all involve situations where the parties "clearly and specifically allocated and accepted the risks associated with future events." *Id.* Thus, the critical inquiry in all of these cases focused on the parties' intent at the time of contracting.

Here, the parties' intent clearly weighs against reformation. As detailed thoroughly above, Luci never intended to accept any part of the SG account and instead sought to cash out in lieu of retaining any interest in the property. Luci made these intentions known throughout mediation. Jay acknowledged and understood these intentions and specifically rejected them. In fact, Jay proudly assumed the risk of the SG account, warning Luci that she would regret not keeping her money in the SG account.

This is clearly a circumstance where the parties intended to cash out Luci and to allow Jay to retain the $300K interest in an obviously risky investment account. The mere fact that Jay's investment failed and did not work out as he predicted is the very "possibility of a future rise or fall in value" that *Nathanson* and *Edwards* have expressly rejected as a basis for reformation. Accordingly, Jay has again failed to meet his burden by clear and convincing evidence that the alleged mutual mistake was one of a present or past fact, and his Motion must therefore be denied.

B. The Parties' and Mediator's Testimony About Statements Made During Mediation Should be Admitted as They Are Offered Only to Disprove Jay's Efforts to Invalidate the Valid and Final Dissolution Agreement and Is Not Offered to Contradict the Agreement or Prove the Amount of Any Claims.

Under Columbia Mediation Rule 2.11, "evidence of conduct or statements by any party or mediator at a mediation session is not admissible to prove liability for, invalidity of, or amount of the claim or any other claim." However, under the Rule, such evidence may be admitted to "prove <u>or disprove</u> fraud, duress, or other cause to invalidate the mediation result . . . in any other proceeding between the parties to the mediation that involves the subject matter of the mediation." *Rule 2.11* (emphasis added).

Jay argues that testimony about mediation communications should not be admitted because: (1) it constitutes information used to prove the amount of the claim; and (2) in the absence of ambiguity, such testimony is inadmissible. Both arguments lack merit.

1. Luci Does Not Seek to Introduce Mediation Communications to Prove the Amount of a Claim

Jay's argument that Luci seeks to introduce the mediator's testimony to "prove the amount of the claim" is simply incorrect. Luci does not seek to introduce the mediator's testimony to prove the amount of any claim. Indeed, Luci is not even asserting any claim. Rather, Jay, the Petitioner, is seeking to invalidate the mediation result and reform the parties' bargained-for agreement on the basis of an alleged mutual mistake. Luci is acting in a purely defensive capacity and seeks to introduce the mediator's testimony only to "disprove" Jay's effort to "invalidate the mediation result" and an otherwise valid and final dissolution agreement. Rule 2.11. Accordingly, Jay's mischaracterization of Luci's purpose for offering the mediator's testimony is unpersuasive.

Moreover, Jay's citation to *Blalock* is unavailing because the facts of this case are wholly dissimilar from those at issue in *Blalock* in which the court excluded the mediator's testimony. In that case, the appellate court concluded that the trial court erred in allowing the mediator to testimony because: (1) the husband called the mediator specifically in an attempt to establish the amount of a disputed claim, in contravention of Rule 2.11; and (2) the mediator's testimony contradicted unambiguous terms in the parties' agreement and the subject promissory note. Neither of these issues are present in this case.

First, as stated above, Luci is not offering the mediator's testimony to establish the amount of a disputed claim. She is offering it to disprove Jay's efforts to invalidate the mediation result and final dissolution agreement. Accordingly, *Blalock* is inapposite on this issue.

Similarly, unlike *Blalock*, the mediator's testimony in this case will not contradict any of the unambiguous language of the Agreement. In *Blalock*, the mediator expressly testified that the wife was entitled to only $23K when the promissory note at issue unambiguously entitled her to $103K. Thus, the testimony was contradictory. Here, however, the mediator is not being offered to contradict any of the express terms of the agreement, but rather to confirm Luci's persistent communications to Jay that the SG account was risky, unreliable, and potentially insolvent. Moreover, as Luci is not challenging the terms of the agreement, but merely claiming that Jay willingly accepted the risk of a future loss on the SG account, Luci has no need to even question the mediator about the express terms of the agreement such that he could even give contradictory testimony. As a result, the rationale for excluding the mediator's testimony in *Blalock* is plainly inapplicable here.

2. Jay's Argument that the Mediator's Testimony is Inadmissible Because the Agreement is Unambiguous Is Incorrect and Represents a Fundamental Misunderstanding of Rule 2.11

Jay also contends that the mediator's testimony is inadmissible extrinsic evidence because the parties' Agreement is unambiguous in establishing the parties' intent to divide assets. This ambiguity argument relies on *Blalock* which, as stated above, involved interpretation of an agreement. Here, that is not the reason for introducing the mediator's testimony. Rather, the testimony again is offered here to show that Jay knowingly and willingly assumed the risk of a future event, i.e., depreciation in the value of the SG account and that he therefore cannot claim mutual mistake as a basis to invalidate the Agreement. Jay's argument about ambiguity is simply a red herring. Finally, the testimony falls squarely within the second sentence of Rule 2.11, which allows such evidence to disprove efforts to invalidate an agreement reached at mediation.

III. CONCLUSION

For all of the reasons stated herein, Jay has failed to meet his burden to prove mutual mistake by clear and convincing evidence, and Luci seeks to offer mediation communications for a purpose expressly permitted under Rule 2.11. Accordingly, the Court should deny Jay's Motion to Modify the Settlement Agreement and to Exclude the Mediator's Testimony.

February 25, 2016   O'Hallaran, Meyer & Jenson

By: *Applicant* _____

Applicant
Attorneys for Respondent,
Lucinda Elaine Minor

PT-B: SELECTED ANSWER 2

O'HALLARAN, MEYER & JENSON
224 COURT STREET
Hamilton, Colombia

MEMORANDUM

TO: Sharon Jenson
FROM: Applicant
DATE: February 25, 2016
RE: Jay Minor v. Lucinda Minor

I. FACTS

Petitioner and Respondent received a dissolution from each other by final decree of this court, dated April 20, 2013. In a Settlement Agreement, the parties divided total assets with an approximate value of $1,200,000. In the Settlement Agreement, Respondent received the main house in Hamilton and her own pension. Petitioner was to receive the vacation home and his own pension, and the SG account. The SG Account, was valued at $500,000. Thus to equalize their shares, Respondent received $200,000 from the main investment account. Each spouse's share totaled approximately $600,000. Both parties were in agreement that the amount in the SG Accounts were worth $500,000 at the time.

Although there was agreement as to the amount of assets in the SG Account at the time, Respondent had long-standing doubts that the investment account would be able to sustain its rate of return. Thus, she agreed with Petitioner for him to take over the SG Account and she would receive cash in the amount to equalize the disbursements. During mediations, Respondent discussed with Petitioner the risks she associated with the account and urged that he too should take his own money out of the account. Though Petitioner had heard similar information as Respondent about the account's riskiness, he decided that he still wanted to maintain his assets in the account.

A year after the mediation agreement, the SG Account crashed after many of the investors began withdrawing their money in full out of the account. Now the assets in the SG Account from the marriage have lost all value. The Petitioner now seeks a reformation of the contract based on mutual mistake. Respondent denies that a mutual mistake was made and asks the court to consider testimony of the mediator in regards to the matter.

II. STANDARD OF REVIEW

Under Columbia Law, settlement agreements in dissolution cases constitute independent contracts, subject to the principles of contract law (*Snyder*). The parties may not seek relief from their own agreement unless they can establish cause sufficient to invalidate the contract. The party seeking to demonstrate any of these grounds bears a heightened burden of proof, and must establish them by clear and convincing evidence. Here, the burden lies with the Petitioner as the party seeking relief from the parties' agreement.

III. ARGUMENT

A. The Mistake as to Future Value of the Funds in the Settlement Account at the Time of the Settlement Agreement Was a Unilateral Mistake Borne By the Petitioner.

Under Columbia law, "To reform a settlement agreement on the ground of mutual mistake, a party must demonstrate that the mistake existed at the time the parties entered into the stipulation." *Snyder*. A unilateral mistake, however, does not constitute a ground for reforming an agreement. (*Snyder*).

Here, the Petitioner claims that both parties were mistaken as to the value of the SG Account at the time the Settlement Agreement was formed. But this is an inaccurate misstatement of the facts. At the time of the formation of the contract both parties agreed that the worth of the assets in the account was $500,000. It is only now that the value of the assets have dropped to nearly nothing that the Petitioner claims that the parties were mistaken and that the assets were actually worth nothing at the time. In fact, the only mistake at the time was in Petitioner's future valuation of the assets.

For a long time, Respondent had resounding doubts about the sustainability of the returns from the SG Account. The returns were well above market but Respondent was wary that such returns could continue indefinitely. While at the time of the Settlement Agreement she agreed with Petitioner that the worth of the assets amounted to $500,000, she had doubts that the value would remain at that amount or that it would grow.

At the time of her dissolution with Petitioner, Respondent was advised by friends that there was reason to doubt the viability of the SG account. In fact, at the time of the mediation, Respondent had heard reliable information that major investors in SG were beginning to cash out their investments. She rightly predicted that the SG account was a risky venture. By the time of the mediation, Respondent no longer wanted any part in the SG Account. Thus, she entered into the settlement agreement with eyes wide open and not based off any false belief of what the SG accounts were worth.

In fact, even the claim that Petitioner was mistaken as to the worth of the SG Account is questionable. At the time of the mediation, Respondent had informed Petitioner about the information she had heard about the SG Account's decline. She communicated such information to the Petitioner and he also admitted that he had hears such information as well. However, he was not swayed by them. The court in *Snyder* held that, "Where information to correct a mistake is readily available, one party may not hold out the mistake as a reason for invalidating the agreement." Here, the information about the risky and potential illegal nature of the SG Account was communicated to Petitioner through more than one source, including Respondent. Nonetheless, Petitioner ignored such information even though minimal diligence would have corrected his mistaken belief of the account's viability. Such willful blindness is insufficient for a finding of a mutual mistake.

Therefore, the court should determine that no mutual mistake was in existence at the time of the Settlement Agreement because it was wholly one-sided in nature.

B. The Existence and Availability of the Funds in the SG Investment Account Do Not Go to Such a Fundamental Assumption of the Agreement Such That There Was No Meeting of the Minds.

In *Snyder*, the court held that "the mistaken fact must form so substantial a premise for the agreement that the stipulation does not represent a true meeting of the parties' minds." Stating further, the alleged mistake must "involve a fundamental assumption of the contract, in the sense that the mistake vitally affected the facts that form the basis of the contract." In *Snyder*, evidence of such a fundamental assumption was shown with evidence that the parties consistently relied on the summaries of the number of shares the estate had in gross instead of net. The number of shares from the summaries was mistaken by both parties to which they continually relied on during negotiations.

In contrast, here the parties did not rely on a mistaken accounting at the time. Instead, they both had a meeting of the minds as to the value of the assets in the SG Account. The assets could have been withdrawn at the time the agreement was made and the Petitioner would have received his expected share of the marital assets. However, he decided not to do such and now bears the consequences of his investment decisions.

The mistake that was present at the time was the future value of the assets in the SG Account. That, however, is not a fundamental assumption of the agreement. In determining the worth of the marital assets, the parties only looked to their present value because the intent was to do an equal distribution of the assets as they currently stood at the time. Future value of assets was an extraneous determination that would require the parties to engage in the exercise of future speculation. Such mental exercise would not aid in the fair and adequate distribution of the current assets as they were presently valued.

C. Reformation of the Agreement is Inappropriate Because the Parties Specifically Allocated and Accepted the Risks Associated with the SG Investment Account.

Under Columbia law, courts do not generally reform dissolution agreements for mistakes relating to future events. (*Nathanson*). The court in *Nathanson* held that, "mistaken expectations about the future are not grounds to set aside or reform a contract--the mistake must relate to a past or present material fact. In determining whether a mistake is about a present or future event, the court in *Nathanson* noted that the critical inquiry must focus on the parties' intention at the time of contracting. If the intention was to allocate risk associated with future events then reformation would not be granted.

Here, the agreement between the parties was an intentional allocation of risk based upon their differing assessments of the value of the SG Accounts assets and the likelihood of future fluctuations in the value. At the time of the agreement the Respondent had expressed her doubts as to whether the SG Account would sustain its current returns. She believed that such high rates of returns were risky and could not be due to effective management of assets. For that reason during mediation, she insisted that the Petitioner take the account.

She did however advise him that he too should question holding the assets because of reliable information she received that the SG Account was unstable. During mediations, Respondent specifically stated that she did not want to take on the risks associated with the SG Account. Petitioner made statements to the effect that he was more than happy to take his chances and that he was confident in the ongoing high returns. In essence, Respondent believed that the SG Account would likely crash in the near future. In contrast, the Petitioner was under the mistaken belief that the account would remain highly productive in the future. This was a mistaken expectation about the future. Thus it is insufficient grounds to set aside or reform the Settlement Agreement.

D. The Statements Made During Mediation Between the Parties Should Be Admitted In Order to Clarify Whether There Was a Mutual Mistake

Under Columbia Mediation Rules, Rule 2.11, evidence of conduct or statements by a party or mediator at a mediation session must not be introduced in order to prove an amount of a claim. However, the rules do allow for admittance of such evidence in order to prove or disprove fraud, duress, or other cause to invalidate the mediation result in the proceeding. Here, by the petitioner's own claim, there is cause to invalidate the mediation result in the proceeding because of the existence of a mutual mistake. The court in *Blalock* defined what "other cause" means stating, "the clear tenor of this list focuses on grounds for invalidation, and includes such grounds as mutual mistake." The court held further that in such cases, parties may avail themselves of the mediator's testimony for purposes of resolving a present issue about the validity of the agreement itself. For this purpose it may seek the court's aid in reforming or rescinding the contract.

Here, Petitioner alleges that there was a mutual mistake as to the worth and nature of the SG Account. Although Respondent does not concede that there was a mutual mistake, it is still the right and responsibility of the court to apprise itself to the statements or conduct that occurred during the mediation in order to resolve whether or not there is cause to invalidate the contract.

Therefore, by the petitioner's own assertion of mutual mistake, introduction of the mediator's statements and those of the parties are admissible.

Furthermore, the court in *Blalock* found that a finding of ambiguity on the face of the agreement is not necessary in cases where there is a claim of fraud, duress, or mutual mistake. It stated that whereas ambiguity merely permits the court to consider other information in interpreting the contract, "invalidation" under Rule 2.11 provides greater grounds for introduction of extrinsic evidence.

E. Introduction of the Statements Made During Mediation Are Not Against Public Policy

Introduction of the statements made during the mediation session is not against public policy. In *Blalock*, the court noted that evidentiary protection for statements made during mediation to court facilitate candor in important negotiations. While this is true, there is also a public policy interest that agreements made during such sessions are upheld and cannot be reformed simply because one party's latent discontent with the results of the agreement. Mediation offers a vital tool to parties and to the courts in resolving disputes. However, such a tool is only as strong as the support it is given. If a party is able to change the terms of an agreement reached through mediation post-hoc, the validity of such agreements will be severely weakened.

Thus, in this instance, the court should allow for the mediation statements to be introduced in order to uphold the integrity of the agreement reached between the parties during mediation.

IV. CONCLUSION

In conclusion, the court should uphold the original Settlement Agreement because there was no mutual mistake between the parties such that the Petitioner is entitled to a reformation of the contract. The court should seek evidence from the mediation session in order to make this determination.

www.ingramcontent.com/pod-product-compliance
Lightning Source LLC
Chambersburg PA
CBHW081732220526
45468CB00008B/2065